DOROTHY EINON'S
Pre-School
Play Book

BLOOMSBURY

Dorothy Einon's
Pre-School
Play Book

Dorothy Einon

First published in Great Britain in 1999
Bloomsbury Publishing Plc, 38 Soho Square, London W1V 5DF

Copyright © 1999 by Dorothy Einon

The moral right of the author has been asserted

A CIP catalogue record of this book is available from the British Library

ISBN 0 7475 4091 8

10 9 8 7 6 5 4 3 2 1

Colour reproduction by Universal Graphics, Singapore
Printed by Delo Tiskarna, Slovenia

When I wrote my first book about children's play, my youngest son was a toddler and his sister had just started nursery school. Together they tested many of the games you will find in this book: in fact, they invented, or reinvented, a few of them. The old favourites are joined here by other games and activities collected from friends, family, nursery schools and playgroups. I hope your children enjoy them as much as mine once did...

Playing with children is surely one of the most delightful things about being a parent. A small child's pleasure is infectious; the seriousness of imaginative play and the delight children show in their own achievements is endearing. For us, these years provide a bank of sweet memories, and although the child will forget the details of the games he plays, he will remember what was learned, the fun it was and the confidence he gained.

By listening and watching children as they play we can often gain important insights into how their minds work. I remember my eldest child flying his toy plane from London Airport (at the bottom of the stairs) to Spain (at the top). When I suggested that it might be easier, and safer, if he moved Spain to the kitchen, he was completely puzzled by my lack of understanding. Spain had to be upstairs because Spain was in the sky. Obvious really – especially to a mind that could only take things at face value. We drove to the airport and flew up into the sky and arrived in Spain. Where else could Spain be? When my younger son excitedly rode his birthday bike into the knee-high mist in our local woods, he asked "Is this another sort of paradise Mum?" I had to agree it was. He is now 6ft 2 in and about to leave for university - but, the memory still makes me smile.

Play, imagination, excitement, pleasure: they all help children learn naturally the things they have to learn, and gain the confidence they must gain. It is fun. If you can encourage your children to carry over the pleasure of playful learning into the more formal structures of school and work, you will have given them a gift which will last a lifetime.

Contents

Contents

Quiet games to play alone

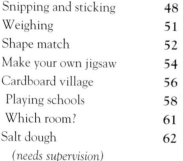

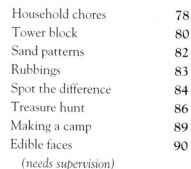

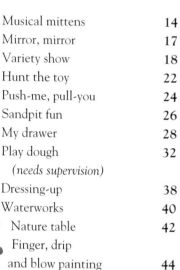

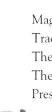

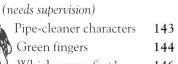

Quiet games to play with others

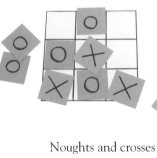

Noisy games to play alone

Noisy games to play with others

The games and activities in this section involve your child in both passive and active play. They introduce him or her to puppets and pretend play, to new and different textures, from sand to play dough, to bright colours, and to a variety of sounds, some musical and some cacophonous. They are all designed both to help his or her development while being fun.

Birth to two years

Musical mittens

Six to ten weeks on

A baby's eye, like his brain, is very immature at birth and his ears work rather better than his eyes. This is why babies love rattles so much. It helps them find objects they want to look at.

This simple but clever idea, a development of the rattle theme, was devised to improve hand-eye co-ordination in handicapped children, but any baby will derive enormous pleasure and benefit from playing it. Try to find some brightly coloured mittens, not necessarily a pair. It's preferable to have them in different colours, perhaps one red and one blue. Sew a bell on to each mitten. Make sure that they are attached firmly so that your baby can't possibly pull them off and swallow them. Scratch mittens are ideal as they come in tiny sizes and it's easy to sew on to the cotton.

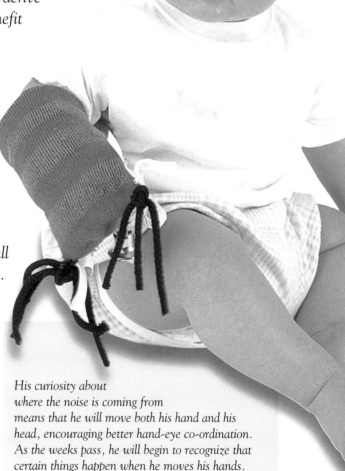

His curiosity about where the noise is coming from means that he will move both his hand and his head, encouraging better hand-eye co-ordination. As the weeks pass, he will begin to recognize that certain things happen when he moves his hands.

Bells
Make the mittens even more appealing by incorporating the bell into a face on the palm side. Use the bell as a nose, or attach two bells for eyes, and embroider the other features, giving the face some hair and a big red smile.

Put on just one mitten to start with, and you should notice that his eyes are drawn to the side from which he hears the tinkling of the bell. The next time you play this game, put on the other mitten to encourage him to look the other way. Use alternate hands every time you play musical mittens, and after several weeks try both mittens at the same time.

Hot weather
If the weather is very hot or your baby doesn't like wearing mittens (some will try to pull them off), thread a bell through a ribbon and tie it around his wrist.

Not just fun but

★ Helps the child locate objects in space.
★ Simple 'I made that happen' game that teaches the child he can influence the world.
★ Locating his hands helps him understand where his body stops and the rest of the world begins.
★ The child must locate his hands before he is able to guide them towards objects.

Tickle me

Six weeks on

Almost all children love being tickled – not too violently of course. Babies in particular love the sensation. The anticipation of being tickled is almost as exhilarating as the action itself. So when you're tickling a baby, build up his anticipation by playing games with him or saying rhymes to him.

Finger rhymes
A natural progression from tickling. At about one year old or whenever he can use both hands together, play 'Pat-a-cake, pat-a-cake, baker's man', and later, when he's able to move his fingers independently, 'Put your finger in foxy's hole', where you trap one of his fingers in your clenched fist, and say, 'Foxy's not at home! Foxy's out chewing a bone' – your cue to chew his finger gently.

Not just fun but

★ A simple cause and effect game for a small baby.
★ Repeated activity and rhyme improves memory.
★ An excuse to laugh and talk.

A catchphrase like, 'Stroke a bunny, stroke a bunny, tickle his little tummy' is ideal as a precursor to a tickle. You can adapt this one to any part of his body, leg, foot, toes, arm, hand. When he's a little older, 'This little piggy went to market' and 'Round and round the garden' will be perfect for engaging his interest and alerting him to the fact that something is about to happen. He should soon be shrieking with glee as he waits for the next tickle, and the game will give you as much pleasure as it gives him.

Mirror, mirror

Throughout two years

A mirror is one of the most appealing and valuable toys for a baby. Not only will she see her own image in the mirror, but it will also catch the light and reflect a rainbow of colours which will fascinate her. At first incorporate a small mirror (the ones used in bird cages are ideal) in a mobile, suspended above her crib. When she is a couple of months old, buy a larger unbreakable plastic mirror, which is safe to hang inside her cot. Place it so that she can see her face close to and catch sight of her movements. Use the little mirror as part of a cradle gym (see page 18). Children do not recognize themselves in the mirror until they are about 21-24 months old.

Not just fun but

★ Provides the stimulus babies love: movement, faces.
★ A cause and effect game. She moves, the image moves.
★ Helps the understanding of self in the second year.

When she is sitting up and aware of her environment, at approximately six months, sit her on your lap opposite a mirror. Talk to her reflection. Point out the parts of her body. Show her how her arms and legs move when you gently pull her wrists and ankles. Wiggle her fingers and toes. Tickle her. Then show her how you move the parts of your body. Pull funny faces. Smile and laugh. She will react. Show her that her reflection moves when she moves her body, but don't expect her to understand.

Variety show

First three months

Y ou can stimulate your baby's interest by collecting a number of different household items to show him every few days. Show him the same ones and introduce a couple of new ones each time. Ideas for appealing objects are given below.

Stretch a piece of elastic, from which you hang objects and toys, across the baby's cot to create a simple 'cradle gym'. Tie the objects on to the elastic or thread the elastic through the holes on the levers of bulldog clips, which you can use to grip the objects.

Not just fun but

Research has demonstrated that babies over six weeks love to look at colourful, noisy objects with strong, clearly-defined patterns. New born babies show more interest in contrast. Black against white is the favourite. They could be cereal packets, postcards, books with vivid covers, seed packets, balls of coloured wool, tightly closed jars containing sweets, beads or marbles that make a noise when you shake them, or your keys which jangle satisfyingly. A new-born baby's eyes are still developing and he can only focus on near objects, so hold yours about 30 centimetres from his face.

★ Gives the child something to look at when in his cot.
★ Simple turn taking activity.
★ Encourages the child to learn the rules of social interaction.
★ Encourages the child to focus and later reach.

Toy on a stick

Two to four months

A new-born baby lacks the visual skills to focus on an object and follow it as it moves. The time to start this activity is when your baby is a few months old and her eyes have begun to track movement. You can encourage this skill by tying a small toy or object to a stick, holding it about one metre in front of her, and then slowly moving it from left to right. Watch her follow the toy with her eyes.

Fix anything that might interest your baby on to the stick – a brightly coloured ball, a little teddy or a basic everyday item such as a metal spoon.

As she improves, take the stick further to each side. Then change the direction and move the stick up and down or towards her and away from her. When she has no difficulty tracking the toy, speed the game up, and finally move the stick diagonally or in a circle.

This activity will improve her head-eye co-ordination, which is poor in new-borns. Their eye movements can't keep up with their head, and you will often see her with her head turned to the side and her eyes, lagging behind, looking in the opposite direction: this is known as 'doll's eye phenomenon'.

Not just fun but

★ Helps the child to focus.

★ Helps the child locate objects in space.
★ Helps her follow objects through space.
★ A simple turn-taking activity.
★ Encourages the child to learn the rules of social interaction.

Musical mayhem

Three months on

There are few activities babies love more than making a noise, and as she gets older, your baby will do this to greater and greater effect. Without shattering your nerves or ear drums, encourage her by providing 'musical' instruments. As soon as she can grip an object, give her a rattle. Choose one in primary colours and made of plastic, which she will like to chew. Babies use their mouths to explore until they can control their hands when they are about seven months old. You can make your own variation on the rattle theme by filling a plastic bottle with a screw top – an old shampoo or bubble bath bottle would be ideal – with a few dried peas or beans. Although not so stimulating visually as the bright rattle, she will appreciate the different sound it makes.

La,

You can use a variety of containers, filled with different things to produce other noises; for example, a tin filled with coins, a small glass jar filled with plastic beads, or a yogurt carton filled with rice.

By the time she is six months old, her co-ordination may have developed well enough for her to be able to strike with a degree of control. Babies of this age love hitting one object with another. This is the time to give her a 'drum'. It doesn't have to be a proper toy drum; she will have just as much fun hitting a saucepan with a wooden spoon. Put on some cheerful background music, to which she can bang and 'sing' along.

La, La... La,

Not just fun but

★ Helps the child locate objects in space.
★ Sounds draw her attention to things she can see.
★ Simple 'I made that happen' game that teaches the child she can influence the world.

★ Hands and the things they hold can be explored with the lips and tongue long before she can use her fingers.
★ Noisy hands are easier to watch.

Hunt the toy

Nine months on

So many of the games which excite babies and make small children laugh involve hiding and seeking. Rest assured that if children find these games fun they must be doing them a great deal of good. So start hide-and-seek games at an early age. The first game you play with her could be to take three clear glasses, preferably plastic, and place a toy under one. Let her watch you do it. Then ask her if she can find it. If she does, congratulate her and tell her how clever she is. Next you could play a slightly more difficult game, where you hide the toy under one of three towels. Once again let her see which one you have put it under. If she finds this game too difficult, leave part of the toy visible. A more advanced variation of this game is to substitute cups or opaque glasses for clear ones, while still allowing her to watch you hide the toy.

From about a year, you could hide the toy in a large carton or wastepaper basket, filled with bits of screwed-up newspaper and encourage her to search for it.

As she grows older, you could replace the screwed-up newspaper in the lucky dip game with wood chips, lentils, chickpeas or rice. You could also bury a 'treasure' in sand (see page 26) or, by the time she's two or three, somewhere in the house, leaving a trail of clues.

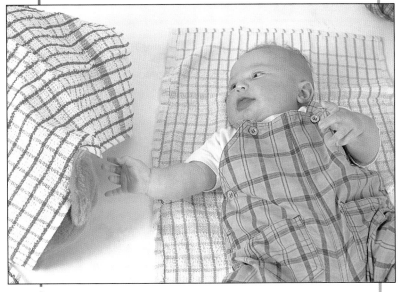

When in doubt we assume understanding. Just think of the way we talk to our pets. In fact small children tend to understand a lot less about things than we think they do. We expect logic and small children are simply not logical. Even though they look for the toy under the glass they may show no surprise if we swop that toy for something quite different when they are not looking. Nor do they always look in the obvious place. If we always hide the teddy under a cloth this is where they will look – even if they have just seen us putting the teddy under a cushion!

Not just fun but

★ Social skills develop while we play together.
★ Encourages turn taking which is a basic communication skill.
★ Improves hand and fine finger skills.
★ Improves understanding of object permanence – learning that objects still exist even when they are hidden.

Push-me, pull-you

From one month after learning to walk

As soon as your child is walking with confidence, he will enjoy playing with toys on wheels which he can push and with toys on a string which he can pull. Pull-along toys are available in the shops in all shapes and sizes, but you can easily make versions yourself, which will be just as much fun for him to play with. To make the simplest version, thread an assortment of household objects – fromage frais or yogurt pots, jam jar lids, cotton reels, large buttons, plastic bottles – on to a piece of soft string or thick wool, about half a metre long. At the top of the string, thread a few beads between two knots to form a handle. If you have a wood, stone or lino floor or a terrace outside, the toy will make a wonderfully satisfying clatter as he pulls it along.

Not just fun but

★ Makes just walking about interesting once the novelty wears off.
★ Simple 'I can do it' game that increases confidence.
★ Improves balance.
★ Encourages the child to walk at various speeds.

Cotton reel version
Use the same soft string that you used for your original toy; again you will need about half a metre. Paint nine or ten cotton reels in primary colours, using lead-free paint. Set the reels a centimetre apart, separating them by a knot or a bead. If the reels are too close together, the snake won't flex. As the finishing touch, make it a plasticine or papier mâché head (see page 96).

Toy cars and trucks are ideal for pushing, but it will take time for him to learn how to push and let go of the toy at the crucial moment. Provide him with a ramp to roll cars down. Do it for him a couple of times, then let him experiment for himself. Once he has learned this skill, remove the ramp and see if he can push them along the floor.

Plastic bottle cart
A pull-along toy will appeal to your child even more if it makes a noise. You can make a jolly-looking cart out of a plastic bottle with a tight-fitting lid, filled with macaroni or coloured beads. Decorate the lid with eyes, nose and mouth, then pierce the nose, so that you can thread the string through. Knot the string, and stick four circles of paper or card on the sides to look like wheels.

Sandpit fun

One year on

Children as young as one year will play happily for hours in a sandpit. Ensure that yours is covered against rain and cats who will use the sand as litter. If you don't have space for an outdoor sandpit, it is still possible to create one inside with a strong cardboard box, an old tyre, a drawer, a baby bath or even a large plastic sheet. Buy the best quality silver sand, which is fine and white. Avoid coarse, low-grade builders' sand, which leaves yellow stains on skin and clothes.

Watchful eye

Fill a washing-up bowl with fine dry sand for your baby to run through his fingers. He will relish its unique texture. Eating sand can be a problem at first and you will have to watch him. Groups of children, playing together, tend to enjoy throwing the sand. This should be firmly discouraged. If sand gets into their eyes, it will be very painful, and you must wash it out immediately.

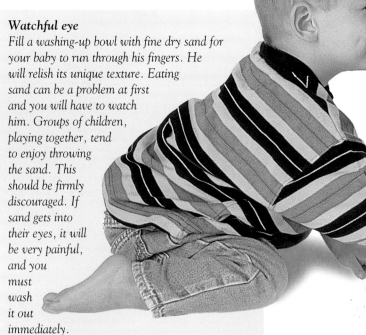

Not just fun but

★ Guaranteed to keep one or two small children amused.

★ Encourages curiosity.

★ Simple science.

★ Encourages the child to work things out for himself.

★ A way to learn about empty and full, light and heavy, wet and dry.

Imagination

Sand invites a child to use his imagination. If he has a stick, he will draw pictures in it. Once he knows his alphabet, he will write letters. Give him a comb or a rake and he will make patterns. You can weigh and meaure, sift and pour the sand, add water and together make wonderful sand pies. You can play a game with him, where you bury a small toy in the sand and ask him to find it; then switch roles and ask him to bury it for you to find.

Have an array of utensils to hand, but don't give them all to him at once. Look out a few of the following: a colander, sieve, funnel, spoon, cup, comb, jelly moulds, weighing scales, plant pots, a bucket and spade and a toy rake.

Dry sand feels quite different to wet sand. Dry sand is perfect for pouring, filling holes and weighing. Wet sand is much better for tunnelling, and for making pies, and castles. If you can, set up a separate box containing wet sand.

My drawer

Eight to 18 months

It's natural for a baby to want her parents with her every minute she is awake, it's natural for parents to need a break. And right too. Everyone needs to learn that sometimes they are first in the queue, sometimes last. The easiest way to negotiate both parents' and children's needs is to let the child play underfoot. Here's a game that fits that bill. It's especially good for those times when you are busy with household chores. But a drawer in the kitchen, a box in the lounge, a waste paper basket in the bathroom also gives you the space to wash your hair, read the paper or make that telephone call.

Babies and toddlers can amuse themselves for hours by simply taking objects out of, examining them, and putting them back into a container. Provide her with a solid, old wooden drawer (check that there are no splinters) or colourful plastic box that belongs to her alone, and fill it with a variety of fun but safe objects and toys. She will find the most basic of things totally absorbing – small children love familiar things.

And after your children have finished with the drawer you may find it useful to keep it around for when friends visit with children.

Not just fun but

★ Develops hand and finger skills.
★ Helps the child learn that objects exist even when she cannot see them.
★ Encourages self-sufficiency – helps her learn to amuse herself.

Fill the draw with things like a pair of socks, a kitchen utensil, soft, plastic and wooden toys. In your selection, try to introduce different textures for her to feel: a soft, fluffy toy animal, a hard plastic rattle or teething ring, a cloth book and a squidgy ball. Find a noisy or musical toy to include, as well as a safety mirror.

As she approaches one year, you could add nesting toys, board books, a pan and a wooden spoon; and at 18 months, she might be ready for a very basic puzzle, a few wooden bricks, a wooden car and some wax crayons and paper.

String bag
If she is an early waker, from one year on you could leave a string bag with some of her favourites from the drawer inside her cot or bedside her bed to give her something to look forward to and to keep her amused in the morning. Change the contents of the bag each night so they will be a surprise for her each morning.

It's an excellent idea to keep her special box until she goes to school or even later, replacing the toys and objects regularly. At five for example, she will be interested in postcards and colourful brochures, stickers, beads to thread, a magnet and a magnifying glass.

Going fishing

18 months on

This is a game my children used to play on Sunday morning while we read – or tried to read – the papers and drink our morning tea in bed. We used to set the game up in the window bay the night before so it was all ready to amuse them.

You need a cardboard box or wastepaper basket approximately 20 centimetres deep. Cover the box or make a cardboard sleeve to fit over the wastepaper basket, decorated with an underwater scene: fish, seaweed, a sandy river or sea bed, in blue water. Draw 10 or 12 fish on card, cut them out, and then put a metal paper fastener through the mouth of each one. To make it easier for children of 18 months to catch the fish, you could use metal bottle tops, painted in fishy colours. But make sure that there are no sharp edges for them to cut their fingers on.

A child who enjoys craft work may enjoy making fishes out of little bits of salt dough (see page 62) or a bit of card and some sticky backed paper. If using the dough embed a bottle top into one side.

Rods and tackle

Cut two pieces of string about 40 centimetres long (one for you and one for him), and attach them to sticks, 30 centimetres long. Pieces of cane or drum sticks will do. Tie horseshoe magnets to the end of the string, stand him close to the box so that he can see the fish and help him to dangle his rod inside. Later you can take it in turns and see which of you can bring home the biggest catch.

Play dough

18 months to five years

Y ou can buy play dough in the shops,
but making it yourself is cheaper and
almost as much fun as playing with
it. You will need two cups of plain flour, one
cup of salt, one cup of cold water with a few
drops of food colouring mixed in (if you add
the colouring to the dough later, you will get
a marbled effect), two tablespoons of oil and
two teaspoons of cream of tartar to make it
last longer. Knead the ingredients together
and then warm them on the stove until they
form a soft lump. Give it to your child while
the dough is still warm. At 18 months, she
will probably be happy just to handle the
dough, squeeze it through her fingers, pound
it flat, pinch it and see it change shape before
her eyes. With your help, she may be able to
roll it into a ball or a long thin sausage. Help
her turn the ball into a fat little mouse and
the sausage into a snake or bracelet.

Not just fun but

★ Making the dough can be
a social occasion.
★ Making the models
allows the child to work by
herself.
★ Self expression through a
creative activity.
★ Encourages the child to
sit still and concentrate.
★ Good for hand-eye
coordination.
★ Good for imitation. She
can make pretend food.

Modelling
As she grows older, she will
become more confident at
modelling. Provide her with
some tools – a rolling pin,
blunt knife, lollipop stick,
pastry shape cutters, stamps –
and some bits and pieces
which she can use to bring
her models to life – straws,
buttons, pipe cleaners, wool,

cocktail sticks, stones. With
your help, she could make
cups and plates for her
teddies, a Noah's Ark of
small animals, or a family of
little figures. If she sees you
preparing food, she might like
to 'cook' with play dough. To
make the food look more
realistic, make up the dough
in different colours.

Casts

Play dough can also be used for making casts. At 18 months, she will enjoy making imprints of her hands and feet. To do this, fill a shallow dish with play dough, two centimetres thick. Help her to press her hand or foot lightly into the dough. Let the cast dry for a couple of days, then finish it with clear varnish. Tree bark is an excellent subject for casts, and an older child could take impressions from a variety of trees in your garden or local park.

Play dough will dry out if left exposed. Store it either in an air-tight container or in a polythene bag in the fridge. If you let it dry out, you can sculpt the hardened dough.

Glove puppets

20 months on

Y ou can make your own simple glove puppet
from an old sock with eyes and lips sewn on –
the mouth can be between thumb and fingers
– see the illustration. Alternatively, buy, or make, a
more elaborate glove puppet. Use it to enliven any
interludes in your daily routine.
Show her what the puppet can do:
wave, pick up spoons, clap, pinch
noses. Invent a personality for
each puppet and stick to it. One
puppet could always be naughty,
and another rude – children love to
be the 'good person' while someone
else is naughty.

Each puppet will
also need its own voice.
This is an activity that will
need an adult's involvement
at the start: show the child
a range of puppet
games. The child
should then copy you.

Getting to enjoy the
glove puppet at this age
will help maximize its
important later benefits:
speech development and
eye-hand co-ordination of a
fairly high order.

★ Learning about the reality of others' points of view. This arises because the child must play several different roles: not only him- or herself, but the puppets' as well.

★ Encourages self-expression.

★ Thinking through what is good and what is naughty.

★ Hand skills.

★ Stretches the imagination.

★ Making up and re-enacting a story exercises memory.

★ Can keep a child amused in boring situations such as car journeys or waiting rooms.

This section, the main part of the book, is devoted to activities which are more demanding of your child's dexterity, hand-eye co-ordination and language skills. They concentrate on make-believe and dressing-up, building, painting and drawing, making things, cooking, movement and growing plants. There are also ball, memory, number, word and party games, and games designed to develop language, listening and mathematical skills.

Two to Five Years

Dressing-up

Two years on

Make-believe is an important part of a child's life between the ages of two and six. Cardboard boxes become cars or castles (see page 140) and, in the 'pretend' games she plays, as the driver of the car or the queen of the castle, the child herself is grown-up. To be a grown-up, she has to dress like one, and a dressing-up box is usually the source of more hours of unbeatable playtime than any toy.

A cowboy costume, a Superman outfit and a policeman's helmet are all fun to wear, but the most successful dressing-up clothes are adult cast-offs. Although flared skirts, lacy nightdresses and full, frilly petticoats will all be invaluable, it's the accessories that will really make her feel the part – a feather boa, patent handbag, high-heeled shoes, broad-brimmed hat, long evening gloves, sequinned belt, jazzy scarf, beads, bangles, earrings and sunglasses.

Some children don't like clothes that have to be pulled on over their heads, so aprons, capes and other garments that can be slipped on are ideal. If you are adapting clothes for the dressing-up box, remember that Velcro is the solution for fastening collars and belts and easy for little fingers to cope with. Make sure that there are no clothes with cords at the neck, and that the skirts are not too long; she will be frustrated if she's tripping up all the time.

Acting stories
If you have a group of children, when they are all dressed up they could enact some of their favourite stories.

★ A social (or solitary) game which encourages conversation with others or with himself.

★ Helps the child's memory. He must match his play to his knowledge.

★ Pretence encourages the child to think about himself and contrast this with his knowledge of others. Psychologists call this the development of a theory of mind.

★ Good for fine finger skills.

Storing

Store your dressing-up clothes in a large box or basket, but keep small items like jewellery in a separate box, as they tend to get buried or lost. Pieces of material, tablecloths and tea towels can all be transformed into headdresses, saris or sarongs. Jumble sales are marvellous sources of old clothes, if you can't fill your dressing-up box from clearing out your cupboards.

Waterworks

Two years on

Most babies adore bathtime, and the love affair with water will probably continue throughout their childhood. Playing with water is exciting but messy. It's not an ideal indoor activity so, if you can, set up your old baby bath or a washing up bowl in the garden – ideally on a stand or solid table so that your toddler doesn't have to bend or squat. It will be safer at this height as he won't be able to fall in. Small children can drown in quite shallow water and should always be supervised.

Not just fun but

★ A guaranteed way to keep one or two small children amused.
★ A game which encourages curiosity.
★ Simple science.
★ Encourages the child to work things out for himself.
★ A way to learn about empty and full, light and heavy, wet and dry.

Bubbles
Look at how objects appear different underwater. Make bubbles underwater by blowing through a straw or by squeezing an empty detergent bottle.

Provide him with a collection of things to play with: a jug, cup, plastic bottle, colander, sieve, funnel, drinking straws, watering can, old detergent bottle, sponge, corks, pebbles, ice cubes, plastic and metal spoons, clothes pegs, rubber ball, marbles and ping pong balls. At first he will be perfectly happy using the containers for pouring, filling and transferring water from one to another, seeing which hold water and which let it out. Then carry out some experiments together to determine which objects float and which sink, and of the ones that sink, how quickly they do it. An older child could make a pictorial chart to show the results.

Boats

Water cries out for boats. He might have a few toy boats, but he can make a fleet of his own with corks, cocktail sticks and the cut-out side of a yogurt carton. Use the cocktail stick as a mast and stick it into the middle of the cork's side. Cut out a third of the yogurt carton and pierce it top and bottom for the sail. Weight the under side of the cork with some Blu-Tack. Paint different coloured numbers on the sails and race the boats across the water, blowing them through straws.

Ping pong balls

These are cheap and make wonderful water toys. Buy about 20 and see how many he can trap underwater with a plastic bucket. Give them to him to play with in his bath. He should be delighted by the way they keep popping up.

Nature table

Two years on

When he starts school, your child will spend hours on walks and in the garden on the lookout for exciting and unusual contributions to the 'nature table'. Before then it is perfectly possible to import this idea into your home, and set up a small table, an upturned crate or a shelf, devoted to his finds from the natural world. The creation of the display will be particularly beneficial to city-bred children, and even for country children, walks will have an extra point to them.

Beach combing

If you have a day at the seaside, you could give your nature table a sea shore theme, with sand, shells, seaweed, pebbles, gull feathers, driftwood and shingle.

Leaves and feathers

On walks, collect as many different leaves as you can find, from both evergreen and deciduous trees. When he sets them out on the table later, he can compare them and you can try and identify which trees they come from (make sure you have a book to help you). You might find feathers (never touch birds' eggs), nuts, conkers and acorns in the autumn, berries (make sure he doesn't eat any), and a variety of mosses. Only pick a wildflower if it is plentiful, and then only one specimen. The same applies to mushrooms and toadstools (make sure he doesn't eat these either, and that he washes his hands after touching them), which you should carry home in a basket not a plastic bag. With paper and a soft pencil, an older child could make bark rubbings from the various trees he finds and include them in the display.

Snails

These are interesting to keep in a small aquarium or a clear plastic box. Feed them on lettuce. They move along their slime trails on little false feet called pseudopodia. Looking from the other side of the clear plastic it is possible to see how they do it. After a three or four days you could take them to the park or eat bake them with a good helping of garlic butter. They need to be boiled for an hour or so first.

Insects

Children are usually fascinated by insects. If he is, collect some specimens to keep on the nature table for a few days before returning them to the garden. Avoid butterflies; some are rare and they suffer from being trapped. Try to catch worms or crawling insects, such as ants and earwigs. Keep them in a large glass jar with holes punched in the lid or muslin stretched across the top and fixed firmly with a rubber band. Put a mixture of sand and soil in the jar with a few stones and leaves from the plant you found the insect on, to provide food.

Not just fun but

★ Sustained activity.
★ Teaches the child to plan.
★ Teaches the child to work by himself.
★ Teaches the child to sit still and concentrate.
★ Many of the collecting tasks involve hand-eye co-ordination.
★ Helps categorization.
★ Teaches the child about nature.
★ Sense of achievement boosts confidence.

Finger, drip and blow painting

Two years on

Art provides one of the most important means of creative expression for a small child. But don't just give him a box of paints and a single brush and expect him to get on with it. He will derive much more pleasure and benefit from experimenting with a range of different materials and techniques.

An old toothbrush dipped in paint is perfect for spray painting. Set him up in your messy corner for this activity. If you place stencils or objects like a leaf or key on the paper, he will produce some stunning patterns.

★ Good for children who have not yet mastered a paint brush.
★ All forms of painting allow the child to work by himself.

★ Self expression through a creative activity.
★ Encourages the child to sit still and concentrate.
★ Good for hand-eye co-ordination.

Printed record

If you want to keep a permanent record of his painting you can take a print. Just place a piece of paper over the paint and press down gently and evenly. A rolling pin works well. If the paint is thick make the first, throw-away, print with newspaper. The second or third print is usually the best.

Supervision

You must supervise his blow painting at the beginning as he may be tempted to drink paint through the straw. By putting the paint on to the paper however, this shouldn't pose a problem.

Finger painting

An excellent way of starting him off is with finger painting. You can buy special finger paint or make it very successfully yourself by mixing one cup of soapflakes, one cup of cold water starch and one and a half cups of cold water. For the colour, add food colouring or powder paint.

Paint needs to be thick for finger painting, so dress him in an overall, cover a plastic tray or board with paint, then let him smother his hands in it. Provide him with thick sheets of paper for him to paint patterns (they might just be blobs of paint, made with one finger), abstract pictures with a splendid mixture of colours, hand or thumb prints.

Drip painting

Some children just don't like getting their hands dirty. If yours is one of them, there are other ways of painting pictures before they are ready to use a brush, such as drip painting and blow painting. Add more water to make the paint runny, and put a blob in the middle of the paper. By picking up the edges of the paper, he can make the paint travel across the paper to form a picture, or with a straw, he can blow the paint across it. When the paint has been absorbed into the paper, pour a different coloured paint on to it and let him blow again.

Indoor picnic

Two years on

Children love small changes to their daily routine, and this idea turns an everyday teatime into a treat. Everyone associates picnics with summer, the countryside, park or beach but, even in the depths of winter, you can cover your living-room floor with a rug and pack up a basket of goodies. To make the picnic authentic, use paper plates and cups (you might spread a waterproof sheet under the rug in case of spills), plastic spoons and forks, and have a damp cloth nearby for sticky fingers.

Finger food is best for picnics, and the children can help you prepare it. You could have a dip with carrot, cucumber and celery sticks; hard-boiled eggs; chicken drumsticks; cherry tomatoes; grapes; and sandwiches, which you can make more interesting by cutting into teddy or dinosaur shapes with biscuit cutters.

There will be hardly any washing up after your picnic and, unlike the real thing, you won't get sand in your sandwiches or be in danger of getting caught in the rain.

Helping

By helping you to get the picnic ready, the children will have an early lesson in how to choose and prepare their own food. Eating finger food on the floor will also be practice for times when it isn't possible to eat a proper meal at a table: a car journey or a day at the seaside, for instance.

Not just fun but

★ Social fun.
★ Simple pretend game for the very young.
★ A good sustaining activity for a wet afternoon.
★ An opportunity to talk.

Snipping and sticking

Two years on

Half the joy of scissors is simply in the cutting, and even two year olds are not too young to have a go. For safety's sake scissors should be blunt-ended and their use supervised. Cut some paper strips approximately 30 cm long and no more than 1.25 cm wide for easy handling and snipping. Provide boxes or bowls for the pieces to land in, and you're ready to start scissoring.

Glues

The best type of commercially available glue is PVA (polyvinyl acetate). It is non-toxic, easy to use and clear when dry. More important it will sponge off most surfaces when newly applied, and can usually be peeled off when dry. A cheap home-made paste can be made according to the following recipe: take one handful of flour, a pinch of salt and add water until gooey. Alternatively, add water to half a cup of flour until it is as thick as single cream. Simmer and stir for five minutes. Add food colour and store in the fridge in an airtight jar.

Gluing

Spreading glue on large sheets of paper or cardboard is just as much fun as with snipping, and two years is not too early to start if the activity is kept to its bare essentials with some adult supervision. You must use a non-toxic glue or a home-made flour paste (see below left). Dress him in an apron – preferably one with sleeves. Add household dye to the glue to make it stand out on the paper, and show him how to spread it evenly all over the sheet with his hands. As he becomes more competent, he could progress to spreading the glue with a sponge or a spatula.

Using simple stencils, help the child to spread the cut-out areas with glue, then sprinkle the glued areas with glitter or paper confetti from his box of cuttings. Shake away the excess and show him the result.

Not just fun but

★ Helps the child to work towards an end.
★ A quiet activity.
★ Doing things together encourages conversation.
★ Teaches the child to follow instructions.
★ Sustained activity.
★ Good fine finger activity.
★ A basic skill which can be built on later.

Odd man out

Two to four years

Start playing a simple form of 'Odd man out' with your child from an early age. If he isn't ready, leave it and try again in a month or so. Its benefits are that it will hone and expand the observation skills that he has been acquiring since birth as well as helping him to categorize things.

Language version

At five or six he might be capable of playing a language version of this game. Instead of showing him the objects themselves or pictures of them, just tell him what they are – a monkey, giraffe, hippopotamus and lobster – and ask him which one doesn't fit (see Categories, page 175).

Not just fun but

★ Observation skills.
★ Understanding categories.
★ Understanding same and different.
★ Encourages language.

Making it harder

At first you don't even need to make 'Odd man out' a formal game: just put two apples and a banana in your fruit bowl at teatime and ask him which one is different. Or put out a plate of chocolate biscuits and include one jammy dodger and see if he can pick it out.

Gradually you can make the game harder. Cut out card shapes and see if he can spot the odd one in a series of, say, two triangles and a circle. When he's older you can introduce shapes as complex as rectangles and ovals, but not yet.

Using pictures of animals, for example, you could have two mammals and a fish or bird. See if he knows which one is different and why. You could have pictures of two flowers and a tree, two articles of clothing and a kitchen utensil, or two pieces of fruit and a tin of soup (two pieces of fruit and a vegetable might still be too hard for him). Use any picture cards you might have or as in 'Pairs' (see page 120) draw your own.

Weighing

Two to five years

Using scales is an integral part of a number of games included in this book: 'Open all hours' (page 106), 'The post office' (page 124), 'The baby clinic' (page 114) and 'Little chef' (page 110). Weighing can also be a worthwhile activity without being part of a game, especially for children of two and three who won't yet understand the concept of weight. At this age, children tend to think that size is the same as weight, so if one object is larger than another, it will also be heavier. It will come as a big surprise when they discover that a potato weighs more than a large bag of crisps. In order to carry out experiments in weighing, you need a set of old-fashioned balancing scales. A toy set will be fine; it isn't necessary to know precise weights, just to be able to weigh one object against another.

Later...
When he's confident about weighing, you could introduce him to your kitchen scales, and help him to understand their readings. Any play with scales and weighing will assist him in maths when he comes to learn the subject at school.

Gather together a selection of things, some light, such as rice and lentils, cereal, plastic toys and buttons, and some heavy, like potatoes, onions, stones, metal toys and wooden bricks. Show him how the scales dip down when you place an onion in one of the pans. Pour some lentils into the other pan, and show him that you will need a great many lentils to balance the weight of the onion. Let him experiment with different objects.

Shape match

Two to four years

During the second year of her life, a child becomes more and more interested in how things can disappear and reappear. At the same time the bones in her wrist are developing and she is able to twist her hand before putting things into place. This skill enables her to make a tower of bricks or use a posting box. At one this skill is quite crude – and is motivated by watching shapes disappear and reappear. By two she can manage four to six simple shapes. The motivation changes from wanting the objects to disappear to wanting to see how they fit.

This game is a more difficult version of a shape sorter which emphasizes the fit rather than the disappearance and is more akin to a puzzle that a shape sorter. It practices both shape recognition and the wrist twisting skills she needs to place accurately.

If the game is too difficult for her at first, you could make it easier by making one of the simple shapes out of sandpaper, another out of a piece of velvet stuck on to card, another out of cork, another out of felt or bubble wrap on card, or any other suitable material you can lay your hands on. Put a little sample of this material inside the outline. Make the outline really bold so it is easy to line up.

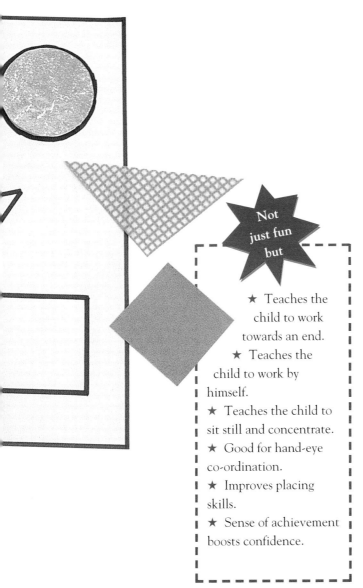

Which shapes?

On a large piece of white card draw a number of different shapes with a black felt tip pen, using strong, clear lines. If you're playing the game with a two-year-old, make the shapes easy – a square, rectangle, triangle, circle, oval and cross – with lots of space between them.

To make it more difficult for an older child, introduce unusual shapes – a hexagon, octagon, rhombus, trapezium, parallelogram, kite and pentagon – and draw them closer together.

From bright coloured card cut out shapes just a tiny bit smaller than the outlines. Match all those that you have drawn. Mix them up in a box and then ask her to place these shapes over the ones on the card. You should make sure she can still see the outline you have drawn when she is placing the shape. The shapes and the recognition of them will help her in the early development of mathematical skills, which she will learn later at school.

Not just fun but

★ Teaches the child to work towards an end.
★ Teaches the child to work by himself.
★ Teaches the child to sit still and concentrate.
★ Good for hand-eye co-ordination.
★ Improves placing skills.
★ Sense of achievement boosts confidence.

Make your own jigsaw

Two to four years

Doing a jigsaw puzzle is an excellent way of making a child concentrate on detail and practise pre-reading skills. It also makes him work through a task until it is completed.

Unless you have the tools and are a skilled craftsman, it's not worth trying to make a proper interlocking jigsaw. Getting the pieces to fit perfectly is just too difficult. In any case, his first jigsaws should be very basic with a few pieces which don't need to lock together.

A game that combines jigsaws and pairs (see page 120), is to cut pieces of card in two. On one half draw a picture and on the other write its name. He has to match all the pieces together.

Not just fun but

★ Teaches the child to work towards an end.
★ Teaches the child to work by himself.
★ Teaches the child to sit still and concentrate.
★ Good for hand-eye coordination.
★ Improves placing skills.
★ Sense of achievement boosts confidence.

sun

kite

ice-cream

candle

fish

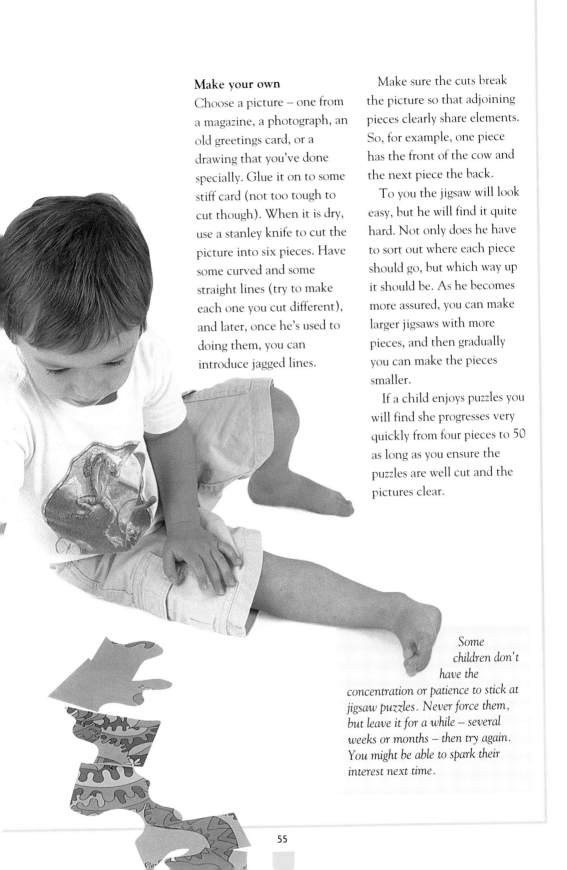

Make your own

Choose a picture – one from a magazine, a photograph, an old greetings card, or a drawing that you've done specially. Glue it on to some stiff card (not too tough to cut though). When it is dry, use a stanley knife to cut the picture into six pieces. Have some curved and some straight lines (try to make each one you cut different), and later, once he's used to doing them, you can introduce jagged lines.

Make sure the cuts break the picture so that adjoining pieces clearly share elements. So, for example, one piece has the front of the cow and the next piece the back.

To you the jigsaw will look easy, but he will find it quite hard. Not only does he have to sort out where each piece should go, but which way up it should be. As he becomes more assured, you can make larger jigsaws with more pieces, and then gradually you can make the pieces smaller.

If a child enjoys puzzles you will find she progresses very quickly from four pieces to 50 as long as you ensure the puzzles are well cut and the pictures clear.

Some children don't have the concentration or patience to stick at jigsaw puzzles. Never force them, but leave it for a while – several weeks or months – then try again. You might be able to spark their interest next time.

Cardboard village

Two to five years

Y ou can make a host of different scenes out
of cardboard boxes – a village, harbour, fort or farm –
but you will need to start collecting cereal
packets, tea bag boxes, toilet and kitchen roll
tubes, fruit juice cartons and egg and shoe boxes
some time in advance. Also save some plastic
containers, like detergent bottles, margarine tubs and
yoghurt, cream and fromage frais pots, which
will give you a range of shapes and sizes.

Construction

First you will have to find a
table where you can build
your village and leave it
permanently. Open up a large
cereal packet, and spread it
flat to form the main road.
Always use the inside of
boxes because it's much
easier to paint and decorate
the natural beige interior.
Make a street of houses and
shops out of little juice
cartons, mini cereal boxes
and the occasional
architectural deviation with a
margarine tub. You could
build a
shoe-box
church with a
yoghurt pot
steeple, and have a silver-foil
pond and a painted cardboard
village green. You can always
introduce objects made from
play dough (see page 32),
papier mâché (see page 96),
salt dough (see page 62),
plasticine or Lego.

Paper clips and fasteners,
hair grips, masking tape,
wool, string, pipe cleaners,
rubber bands and PVA glue
are all invaluable for sticking
your village together. When
the glue is dry, help him to
paint his village with poster
paints (don't forget the road
markings). Let him add some
of his toy cars and little
people and make some salt-
dough ducks to inhabit the
pond.

It is sometimes difficult to
get the completed box-
buildings to stand up on the
carpet. If this is a problem it
is worth using a piece of
hardboard as a base board. It
can be painted to fit in with
the scene. Keep storage in
mind. Something that will fit
under a sofa or on top of a
wardrobe is usually best.

He could set his village by
the sea and sprinkle sand
over plasticine for the shore
and add some shells and
seaweed. Make some little
boats (see page 98) and a
jetty from lollipop sticks
glued together.

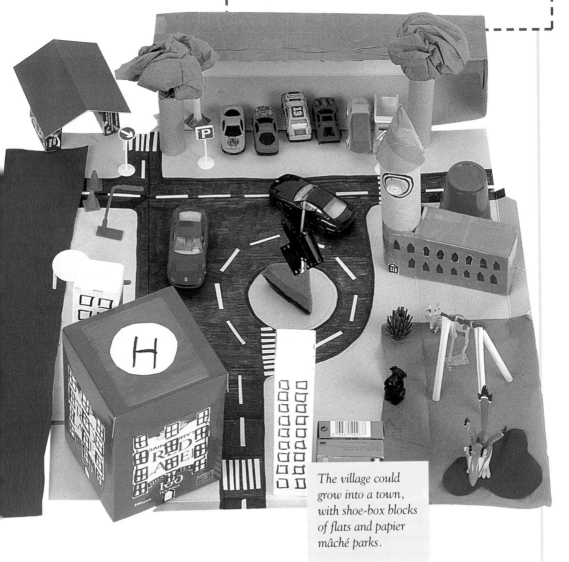

The village could
grow into a town,
with shoe-box blocks
of flats and papier
mâché parks.

Playing schools

Two to five years

Children under four find it
difficult to explain a story line,
(and even to follow one through
by themselves) so when they play
together they need to share a
common experience. This is why
TV programmes and domestic
scenes figure so large in early
pretend play. When life moves
outside the domestic scene so do their
pretend games. So this is an ideal
game for a child who has just started
nursery or school. A younger child
can be carried along on her big
sister's imagination and may even play
a simple version by herself once she has
learned the rules.

You and she should take it in turns to
be the teacher. She will certainly enjoy
being in charge for some of the time.

More props
*You could establish a small
library or reading corner with
a collection of suitable books,
and you could have an art
and craft corner, where she
paints, cuts out and glues
(see page 96). Encourage her
to hand out books, paper and
pencils and to rub out the
writing on the blackboard at
the end of the game.*

*Like the 'Kids' café' (see page
136), your school could be
peopled by real
children if
there are
enough of
them or
toy
animals
and
dolls.*

Make some wall charts (see page 75) and put up some of her paintings to decorate your 'classroom'.

Props

You will need a small table and chairs, a blackboard and some chalk, exercise books, paper, pencils, rubbers, rulers, crayons, paints, paper clips, rubber bands and PVA glue. You could hang your paper plate clock (see page 132) in the classroom, and if you have a bell, ring it to indicate the end of lessons. Bring a globe or map of the world into the classroom for geography lessons, write up some letters on the blackboard for her to copy into her exercise book, or do some simple sums.

Taking turns

When you are the teacher, you could read the class a story. When she is the teacher, she could tell the class one. You could sing songs, do music and movement and have a gym lesson. At the end of the morning, you could ring the bell for lunch. Pack a lunch box for her before you start playing the game and she can eat a picnic at the table just like many real schoolchildren do.

Not just fun but

★ Thinking about what happens at school improves memory.
★ Putting events into sequence is an important skill. It is always easier to do if you have the props to remind you what comes next.
★ A little world helps children to tell a story.
★ Pretend play helps children understand that other people have separate thoughts and feelings.
★ 'Teaching' her dolls is a fun way of practising the skills she learns in school.
★ When children play through their experiences they also play through what they have learned.

Blow football

Two to five years

Young children find it easier to blow through a straw than to suck through one, so they should be capable of playing this game from quite an early age. It is a game for two: you and your child sit on either side of a table. Unless it is a very small table, sit across the width not its length as she won't be able to blow more than about one metre.

How to play

You will need a ping-pong ball, a drinking straw each and something to represent the goals. You could stick ice-cream cartons on the table with Blu-Tack or simply place strips of paper or material about 20 centimetres apart at each side.

The object of the game is to blow the ping-pong ball through your straw and into the goal on your opponent's side of the table while she is trying to do the same. Once she has mastered the skilll of directing the ping pong ball, you will find that the battle is a pretty even one.

Not just fun but

★ Helps breath control.
★ Playing and laughing together forges friendships.
★ Helps spatial skills.

Which room?

Two to four years

Playing this kind of game with children is first and foremost an excuse for conversation. Where does this go? Where would you find that? Even when the child plays by himself, he will probably chatter. Go through all the old interior decorating magazines you can lay your hands on, and cut out pictures of pieces of furniture – a sofa, armchairs, coffee table, dining table and chairs, kitchen table, bed, wardrobe, dressing table – and things that you have around the house from a bath, basin and washing machine to towels, kettle, scales and a range of other kitchen utensils. Concentrate on items that you know will spark your child's interest.

Next find and cut out pictures of rooms from the magazines: a sitting room, dining room, kitchen, bedroom, bathroom, as well as garage and garden. To make the game simpler for a very young player, just have three rooms: sitting room, kitchen and bedroom. Stick the room pictures on the front of cardboard folders. Then lay the pictures on a large table and encourage him to help you put all the pieces of furniture and objects in the right rooms or folders.

If you're playing 'Which room?' with a two-year-old, you may find it best not to bother with the folders, stick the pictures of your three main rooms on cardboard and place them in front of you both on a table. Then ask him to put the furniture and objects in, or rather on, the correct rooms.

Not just fun but

★ Improves observational skill.
★ Sorts objects – a pre-mathematical skill.
★ Any excuse to talk is a good.
★ Placing skills help hand-eye co-ordination.

Salt dough

Two to five years

This material, not nearly so well known as play dough (see page 32), is terrific for modelling. It hardens when dried in the oven, after which it can be painted and varnished. Pieces made from salt dough look surprisingly professional, yet it is very simple to make.

Mix together three cups of plain flour, one cup of salt, one cup (or slightly more) of cold water and one tablespoon of glycerin. Knead the dough to get rid of the air, until it has an elastic consistency.

Name plate
Help him to make a name plate or initial for his door out of salt dough. Make the plate first, then make the letters and add them to the plate. Press a paper clip into the top for a hook.

Modelling

Now the dough is ready to be modelled. If your child is two or three, he will enjoy rolling it out flat with a rolling pin and using pastry cutters to make shapes, figures and animals. Use a knitting needle to make a small hole in the top so that you can thread a piece of ribbon or string through it to hang his model up.

Older children could model an object, animal or character, free-hand. Cover a flat baking tray with silver foil and, when the model is ready, place it on top and pop it into a fairly low oven (pre-heated to about 150 degrees Centigrade) to bake it dry. You are not trying to cook the dough. If the oven is too hot, you will burn the outside and leave the inside soggy. Flat figures will probably need about one and a half hours in the oven; three-dimensional models will take longer. Remove the model from the oven to cool, then let him paint it with water colour or poster paints. Allow it to dry, then he can varnish it.

Finishing

If he doesn't wish to paint the model, bake it to a lovely honey-brown colour which, when covered with a clear varnish, will look stunning.

Not just fun but

★ Making the dough is a social occasion.
★ Making the models allows the child to work by himself.
★ Self-expression through a creative activity.
★ Encourages the child to sit still and concentrate.
★ Good for hand-eye co-ordination.
★ Sense of achievement boosts confidence.

Buttons

He could make tiles, buttons and beads from salt dough and, if you have the pins, brooches too.

Going abroad

Two to five years

When my eldest son was small he firmly believed that some place 'abroad' was up in the sky. He had of course travelled there by plane. Around holiday time it's fun to transform everything to do with the holiday into a pretend game. This one involves a travel agency – but you could equally set up a hotel front desk or a little world of tents.

The area that you use for a shop (see page 106) or a post office (see page 124) needs to be transformed into a travel agency. Pick up as many different brochures as you can from local travel agencies to stock your make-believe one. Let her be the customer first while you take on the role of the agent, trying to sell her a holiday.

Take-off

Once she has decided on her destination and bought her ticket from you, she will need a passport. Help her to make a simple one from a piece of card. Draw a box inside and tell her to draw a picture of herself in it to look like a photograph. Opposite write, 'My name is', underneath it, 'My hair is', and underneath that, 'My eyes are', with boxes next to the phrases. If she can't yet write her name, write it in the box in faint pencil for her to write over. She can colour in the boxes for her hair and eye colour with a crayon.

She could travel abroad by train or aeroplane. Line up some chairs to make the journey more realistic. You might even become an air hostess or steward and bring her a little tray of food.

When she arrives, if it's a beach holiday, she might like to put on her swimsuit, sunglasses and a sunhat and play on 'the beach'. You could put beach towels out in your playroom to create the right atmosphere.

★ A social game which encourages conversation.

★ Helps the child's memory. She must match her play to her knowledge.

★ Pretence encourages the child to think about herself and contrast this with her knowledge of others. Psychologists call this the development of a theory of mind.

★ The props of a pretend game help her to juggle ideas.

★ A sustained activity that can keep children amused for long periods.

Colour sorting

Three to four years

To learn what the word red means the child must understand what a red shoe, a red bus and a red ice lolly have in common. This is hard because you cannot point at red without at the same time pointing at something else. Children begin to see colour soon after they are born and can match things that are the same colour as soon as they understand the task.

You need an egg box for this activity. To start with, use a six-egg box and, when you want to make the game more complicated, you can progress to a 12-egg one. Cut the lid off so that you're left with the base, and paint or colour with felt tips the inside of the egg holders. Use strong, clear, easily differentiated, colours like red, blue, yellow, green, black and white.

For two-year-olds use saucepans or shoe boxes and make sure none of the objects can fit into the child's mouth.

When she's ready to move on to a 12-egg box, you can paint the egg holders in a range of different and more difficult colours such as orange, purple, pink and two colours the same, but one dark and one light.

Not just fun but

★ Helps the child understand the concept of colour.

★ Matching and sorting underlies many mathematical ideas.

★ A quiet repetitive game when the child needs a period of calm.

In a shoe box collect small miscellaneous items – not too tiny if she's only three, but small enough to fit inside the egg holders – in the six colours that you've used to paint the egg box. Find some beads, buttons, hair slides and marbles, and make some balls from screwed-up coloured paper. Sit her down at a table with the egg and shoe boxes in front of her. She must pick something out of the shoe box, look at the colour and place the object into the correct egg holder. Show her how to do it the first time and encourage her to say the name of the colour as she does it.

Fit the lids

Two to five years

Matching skills are at the very heart of understanding what numbers mean. To understand the 'fourness' of four the child has to see what four teapots and four cups have in common. Matching lids to jars, boxes and other containers requires no special equipment, just some objects you're bound to have around the house. If she's only two, find three or four things with lids that fit on easily like a saucepan, beaker and a shoebox. Seat her at a table and place the empty containers and their lids in front of her. See if she can match which lid fits which container – help her if not – and then see if she can fit them on.

Get her to count the jars and the lids once she has finished – then take off the lids and count them all again. It helps to make the message clear!

When she's older, fill a shallow box or tray with ten or 12 empty containers of different shapes and sizes with different kinds of lids that screw on, slide on, press on or in: film containers, yoghurt pots, jam or spice jars, bottles with stoppers, ice-cream cartons, small tins and boxes. Again, she has to match the lids and fit them on to the containers. When she becomes adept at this, you could make the game even more difficult by choosing containers which all look similar and are the same size.

Not just fun but

★ Matching also plays a role in reading. The child needs to understand that a particular set of letters match a particular spoken word.
★ Eye-hand co-ordination is improved.
★ Improves concentration.
★ Helps the child with work with better sense of organization – especially with the more difficult tasks.

Pin the tail on the donkey

Two to five years

A party game that is too amusing to be kept in a box for the rest of the year, this is really a game for a crowd, but can be played with two. Draw a large picture of a donkey on thick card. Draw separately and cut out a card tail, and stick some Blu-Tack at the top of it or you could use a pin. Laughter binds a social group and breaks the ice. The message to get across is that it does not matter if the child gets the tail on the donkey or not. If the game has got a bit competitive it could be time for you to demonstrate how best not to do it.

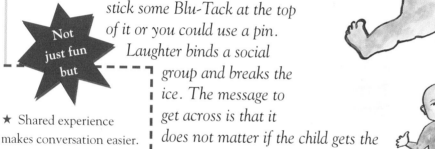

Not just fun but

★ Shared experience makes conversation easier.
★ Understanding words like nearer and nearest.
★ Improves balance and co-ordination.

Variations

If you grow bored with pinning the tail on the donkey, you can make subtle changes to the game without spoiling the fun. You could pin a curly tail on the pig, pin the moustache on the man or pin the nappy on the baby. The principle is the same for all versions. The game is guaranteed to bring a party atmosphere to a wet afternoon.

How to play

Use a soft cloth, tied loosely, to blindfold each child in turn. Spin them around once and push them gently in the direction of the donkey. If they're five or six, you could spin them around two or three times. The children all have a go at putting the tail in the right place on the donkey. Write the children's names on coloured stickers and stick them on the picture in the places where they make their attempts. The one that's closest to the right spot is the winner.

There will be much hilarity when the children see where some of the tails end up: from the donkey's nose to between his eyes.

Button box

Two to five years

There are times when all your child needs is a simple activity and this activity usually provides the solution.

Try to collect as many different buttons as you can because she will enjoy examining them all closely. She will also spend time fingering them, so see if you can find buttons with different textures for her to feel: ones that are covered in velvet or other material, leather, pearl, gilt, plastic or wooden buttons. Have a range of different sizes, colours, shapes, simple and fancy ones. Avoid tiny buttons as they will be too hard for her to pick up, and are too easy for her to insert into her mouth, nose or ear when you're not looking.

Not just fun but

★ Matching and sorting underlies many mathematical ideas.

★ Seeing what things have in common underlies the child's ability to form concepts.

★ Helps the child understand that things can be arranged in sequences such as from small to big.

★ Helps colour naming.

★ Looking for small differences between buttons employs the same skill as looking for small differences between words.

★ Good for fine finger skills.

Ways to play

Help her to sort them. Make groups of buttons that are identical for instance, or the same colour, or small and large ones, patterned and plain ones, round and unusual shaped ones. You could change your categories each time you play with the button box.

Look out some containers for her to fill with buttons – she could use a spoon as a shovel – or scales so that she can weigh them. When she's older, she could thread a number on a piece of wool to make a button necklace or use them in collages (see page 98).

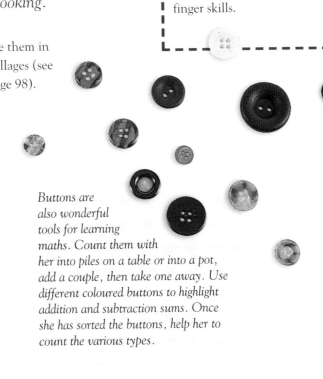

Buttons are also wonderful tools for learning maths. Count them with her into piles on a table or into a pot, add a couple, then take one away. Use different coloured buttons to highlight addition and subtraction sums. Once she has sorted the buttons, help her to count the various types.

Skittles

Two to five years

As well as introducing your toddler to some 'Safe indoor ball games' (see page 74), let him try playing skittles. As with first ball games, playing skittles will help him to learn how to aim. It will also involve him in counting. You don't need a proper set of skittles. You can play with plastic bottles or the cardboard tubes inside kitchen paper. Balance them on Lego bricks if they are too stable to knock down easily.

This is also a good task for teaching the child his colours. Just paint the cartons with poster paint or stick coloured paper tape on the bottle tops.

Skittles lends itself to being played by a group of children, which will introduce an element of competition into the game. Who will knock down the most skittles? Counting will be even more important, and you may have to act as referee.

Not just fun but

★ Throwing or rolling is a difficult skill which needs lots of practice.
★ Improves eye-hand co-ordination
★ Taking aim teaches the child to plan movements.
★ Improves spatial skills.
★ Helps the child with counting and colour naming.

Options

To start with, use only three or four skittles and stand him about a metre away. Find a large soft ball for him to roll at them, or use a newspaper ball or a pair of rolled-up socks. He can throw the ball if he likes, but encourage him to roll it if he can. Increase the number of skittles and the distance he stands from them, the more practised he becomes. If he succeeds in knocking down one skittle for example, explain to him that he has two skittles left. Explain the arithmetic to him every time he plays a game.

Who lives in this house?

Two to five years

At this age children do not know how to play games which involve logic or strategy. This is a simple variation on a board game which is easy to make and it is useful for teaching a child the names of animals and the places where they live. You have to make eight or ten 'houses' out of pieces of folded card. Don't be too ambitious: draw simple pictures of a kennel, stable, hutch, mouse-hole, nest, burrow, hive, sty, hen-house, lily pad. In all the 'houses' cut out a doorway or flap through which the animals can enter their homes.

If she enjoys this game, extend it to include all kinds of other animals – a badger and set, fox and earth, bear and den. You could also use 'Who lives in this house?' to teach her the names of the male, female and young of each species, and to discuss wild and domesticated animals.

Not just fun but

★ Matching is an important pre-maths skill. It helps the child see what three animals and three homes have in common.
★ Expands the child's vocabulary.
★ Quiet game, with the added advantage of imaginary play.

The animals

Next try and find a toy for each of the animals – dog, horse, rabbit, mouse, bird, mole, bee, pig, chicken, frog – either small soft or plastic ones. If you don't have a toy, you could make an animal out of play dough (see page 32), salt dough (see page 62) or plasticine or, failing that, draw one on card and stand the card upright in a piece of moulded plasticine. Line up the houses on a table, and then present her with your animal collection. She has to work out which animal lives where.

Hissing Sid

Two to four years

Push-along toys are easy to cope with – even for those new on their feet. Dragging something beside is more difficult – behind is easier, as 'Hissing Sid' should show.

A basic cardboard snake is quick and easy to make and it can then be decorated as stylishly or simply as you want. All you need is a longish piece of string, half a dozen or so empty toilet roll tubes and some sticky tape.

With cotton reels
She could also make an effective snake from painted cotton reels, which will clatter reassuringly along a hard floor as she pulls it behind her.

Not just fun but

★ Encourages balance.
★ A simple cause and effect game.
★ Fine finger skills.
★ Working towards an end (if the child makes the snake).
★ Encourages the child to sit still (while making the snake).
★ Helps the child play and laugh at scary things.

Thread one end of the string through a tube and then double it back and tape it securely to the outside of the tube. Then thread the remainder of the tubes on to the string. Turn the free end into a handle, and you're ready to decorate.

With crayons you can draw in stripes or scales, with paint give him exotic patterns and slit eyes, or with coloured paper you can really go to town and make a snake to grace a carnival.

ABC scrapbook

Three to five years

P utting together an alphabet book is an activity that you and your child can do quietly together. He may already know the alphabet and be able to come up with many of his own ideas for pictures, but it won't matter if he hasn't yet learned it. He will depend more on you at first but, after a few sessions on the scrapbook, he will start recognizing letters by himself.

Buy a large scrapbook with at least 26 pages, and at the top of each page write a letter of the alphabet. Write the letter twice, using both the upper and lower case versions. Then gather together some magazines, brochures and postcards, and put them out on a table with drawing paper, felt tips, scissors and glue. Sit side by side at the table and start with A. Ask him if he can think of anything beginning with A. If he can't, help him. If, for example, he says,

'Arrow', see if you can find a picture of one. If not, draw one yourself and stick it in the scrapbook. Try and find three or four more pictures of objects beginning with A before you move on to B.

Don't attempt to do too many letters at once – just two or three at a time – or it will confuse him and be detrimental. Whenever you're stuck for something to do, get out the ABC scrapbook and tackle a few more letters.

Not just fun but

★ Helps with letter recognition and naming.
★ Helps the child to pick out the initial letter of many objects.
★ Sticking in pictures improves hand-eye co-ordination.
★ Working towards an end.
★ Learning to sit still.

Safe indoor ball games

Two to five years

E ven if you are confined to a small apartment, it can be great fun playing 'ball' games with a young child. Make balls from rolled-up newspaper. Clear all delicate and easily breakable objects from the room. Using a rolled-up newspaper as a bat, you can play 'cricket'.

With more than one child, you can have competitions to see who can throw farthest, or throw the 'ball' into a wastepaper basket at varying distances.

Not just fun but

★ Hand-eye co-ordination.

★ Muscle and limb control.

★ Playing together.

★ Using both hands together.

★ Improves the timing of actions. Hands must be in the right place when the ball arrives.

Wall charts

Two years on

Charts are more than room decorations, they provide a talking point for the day's activities. Use them to record daily events – always a good conversation opener – daily weather or something much longer term like the height of the sunflower or even the child himself. My children liked to record the weather on a chart – we made symbols to show sun and rain and recorded the temperature every lunchtime – we then talked about what we could do on wet or windy days (see also page 158).

Not just fun but

★ Something to talk about.
★ Recording events helps the child remember – and this in turn helps him to tell the story of his day.
★ School work needs organization and this is good practice.
★ Excellent for memory, language and the organization of ideas.
★ Charts can be set up so the sequence of objects or events depicted on the page are presented like words. Left to right and top to bottom. This helps to teach the child where he should start reading on the page and which direction to go in. Something that is obvious to us – but not to a small child.

Options

Depending on what sparks his interest, your chart could depict car badges, or dinosaurs, insects, fish, vegetables, fruit, trees or wild flowers. Another idea is to keep a wall-chart diary. Have a square for each day of the week, and at the end of the day ask him what he has done on that day. He might say, 'Nothing' or that he can't remember, in which case prod him: ask him what he did at playgroup or had for lunch. When he tells you, write a sentence in the square for that day and get him to illustrate it.

Another possibility is to make a chart of expressions. Draw a series of faces showing different moods: happy, sad, grumpy, frightened, confident, sleepy, angry, cheeky, excited, jolly, tearful, laughing, and many others that you will think of yourself.

Blowing bubbles

Two to five years

There is something magical about bubbles as far as young children are concerned. Making your own bubble mixture is cheap and easy and, with a little imagination, you can produce a homemade blower, which will work better and blow more interesting bubbles than one you can buy in the shops. If you can, set up the bubble bowl outside, otherwise in your messy corner with a plastic sheet underneath.

The mixture has to be quite concentrated. Add one cup of washing-up liquid, two cups of water and one teaspoon of glycerin. Make a blower from a piece of wire or pipe cleaner. Form a loop at the top and twist the wire into a straight handle. She can also blow big bubbles through a funnel or a straw stuck into the bottom of a foam cup.

To make huge bubbles, pull the bottom of a wire coathanger down so that it makes a square shape. Make three times the amount of mixture given, go outside and let her dip the hanger into it by the hook. Leave it there for a few minutes, then tell her to twirl around, with the hanger held upright, and watch the bubble form. Try and do this on a paved area, - the detergent kills grass.

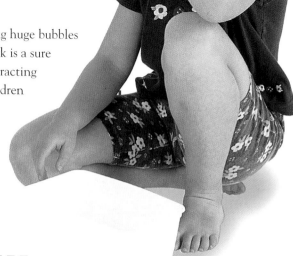

Not just fun but

★ Blowing improves breath control which is good for speaking and singing.
★ A simple cause and effect game that helps children understand they can make things happen.
★ Chasing the bubbles improves spatial skills.
★ An excuse for wonder and laughter.

★ Making huge bubbles in the park is a sure way of attracting other children and making friends.

Heads and bodies

Two to five years

When men need to break the ice they usually tell a joke, women just talk. I'm never sure how much this is a cultural norm and how much it is in the nature of men and women, but if the boys in my family are anything to go by the differences start early. Long before they understand jokes small boys love games with a silly angle. Heads and bodies is one of these. To play you must first collect as many pictures as possible from magazines, brochures and on postcards of people and animals. Try to find ones that are fairly uniform in size, and a figure, standing upright, will be the most effective. Then buy a spiral-bound notebook and cut the pages in two horizontally so that you have an upper and lower half. Cut all the pictures in half and stick the top part on one of the upper half-pages (make sure that it is right up against the bottom edge) and the bottom part on one of the lower half-pages (right up against the top edge). Make sure that you centre the pictures carefully across the width of the half-pages, so that the halves all match up.

When you have filled the book, you will have a collection of the most bizarre looking creatures, and by flipping over the half-pages you will be able to create many more. Give it to your child, who will be delighted and amused by the combinations he can create. See if he can match the correct top and bottom halves to make the proper figures.

Not just fun but

★ Observational skill.
★ Conversational starting point.
★ Helps the child look for detail.
★ Makes the child laugh.

Draw your own
You – or, if he's old enough, he – could make an even more successful book by designing your own pictures for it. By doing this, you can make them all the same size and draw people and animals which are an appropriate shape.
    Don't try and make the animals naturalistic. It will work better if you have them standing on their hind legs, and look funnier if you dress them in clothes with shoes, hats, bags and any other accessories from spectacles to feather boas.

Household chores

Two years on

Young children usually love helping around the house. Housework is not a chore for them; it's fun. Even if you think he might be more of a hindrance than a help, don't put your child off, spend some time showing him what to do and organizing any equipment he will need – dusters, a broom, dustpan and brush, washing-up bowl full of warm soapy water, a scrubbing brush, wet cloth, mop and sponge.

When I was a child I loved to polish my Grandmother's wooden floors by sliding around in old woollen socks – a game my children enjoyed too.

Polishing

This is often a favourite pastime for two- and three-year-olds. Set him up at a table with a couple of dusters and give him some silver objects, if you have any, and a pair of shoes. Don't give him any polish, just ask him to rub them with a duster until they shine. Avoid giving him china objects or anything else breakable.

As they're drawn to water, children love washing. It could be washing dishes or clothes.

Not just fun but

★ Teaches the child that families work together.

★ Shows the child that we should all do things for each other.

★ Letting him help is hard work now – but it's a good habit to start.

★ Following instructions and working towards an end encourage skills he will need in later life.

Other 'chores' he might enjoy include sweeping the floor with a broom or carpet sweeper – when he has finished he can clear up the bits with a dustpan and brush, and dusting with a feather duster – keep him away from precious ornaments though.

Look out some plastic utensils, plates and cups for him to wash up. Alternatively show him how to scrub chopping boards with a scrubbing brush, or wash his dusters and some small articles of clothing. If you think putting him in such close contact with water is a recipe for disaster, give him a damp cloth or sponge to wipe the kitchen table or bathroom tiles, or a squeedgy mop to wash down the kitchen floor.

Tower block

Two years on

At a certain age children will pile up anything they can into a tower. All the better to knock it down. Such building was the scene of one of those 'near misses' that I suppose all parents have. My father used to brew his own beer and one Christmas my son got into the cupboard we called the brewery and started to build castles with the bottles. Needless to say the tower fell and several bottles exploded. Quite how he managed to escape with just two small cuts to his arm and chin I don't know. It certainly did not stop him building.

Don't let this activity's simplicity fool you into underestimating its value. Start her off with just a few bricks; three or four is plenty for first experiments. Suggest the idea of a tower by putting a brick on some raised structure – say a box. Then show her how to put one brick on top of another and, once in a while, build up a tall tower so that she can have the fun of knocking it down. Leave her to experiment with the three or four bricks, and don't expect much progress – unless you have a budding architect on your hands. Go back to the bricks with her from day to day, and slowly introduce more bricks and different building methods. Show her, for instance, how to make a much more stable tower by arranging four bricks in a square.

Colour, shape and size

For the pre-school years, colour is less important than shape and size. The bricks should fit together well and be to scale so that the large ones are multiples of the small. This not only makes building less frustrating but teaches her about volume, size and elementary multiplication.

Storage

Make sure that she has about 60 bricks in her set, including some pillars and arches. Store them in their own container: ideally a drawer or a box on wheels, but a strong wastepaper basket or drawstring bag will do. Avoid keeping them in a general toy box, where they tend to get lost.

Not just fun but

★ Simple practice of the hand grip.
★ Learning to let go.
★ Placing is a hand-eye skill.
★ Toppling towers teach her that she can make things happen.

Variations on a theme
- Let the sand run out into a heap.
- Catch it in a cup and let the cup run over.
- Swing the cone to make patterns on a tray.
- Fit a piece of paper into the tray and paint patterns on it with a glue stick. 'See how the sand sticks.' Or explore what happens if the child paints water-lines on the paper.
- Ask the child to make a long, straight, even line of sand out of doors on a flat surface, connecting two imaginary points. This is hard for a small child, but a useful challenge for an older one.

Sand patterns

Three to five years

Here is an interesting variation on familiar sand games inspired by the sand paintings of the American Indians. Make a large cone from card with a tiny hole at the apex and attach string to holes near the mouth of the cone. Suspend the cone apex-down from the edge of a table, or from a shelf, and place a large tray covered in dark paper beneath it. With your finger over the hole, fill the cone with sand. The child can then swing the cone slowly over the paper and make patterns. If she wants to stop at any time, simply put a large saucepan under the cone to catch the sand; refill when she wishes to start again. To make the patterns more interesting, use sand in different colours.

Not just fun but

★ Asking 'Why?' or 'What happens if...' and finding the answers.
★ Improving observation, an essential pre-reading skill.
★ Understanding how patterns are built up.
★ Experimenting.
★ Seeing how the contraption can magnify a small movement of the hand. This could set her thinking in a mathematical way.
★ Hand-eye co-ordination.

Rubbings

Three to five years

As soon as a child can hold a stubby wax crayon, she can make rubbings, an activity based on the same principle as brass rubbing. Anything with a textured surface, either raised or depressed in parts, is suitable: coins, bark (see 'Nature table', page 42), leaves, shells, sticklebricks, embossed wallpaper, a book or greetings card with raised lettering, and any object with an inscription or engraving. Once she has chosen her object, all she will need is a sheet of paper and a wax crayon or soft lead pencil with which to shade over the object.

Some games need lots of space and equipment, others can be played at the kitchen table, on a plane or in the doctor's waiting room. This is one of the best small scale games.

Like tracing (see page 113), rubbing is an excellent precursor to drawing and will help your child to learn to hold a pencil properly. She won't need the same degree of finger control for rubbing as she will for tracing so it she can start the activity earlier.

You can create objects from which she can make rubbings by cutting out cardboard shapes and pictures, letters and numbers and sticking them on to a piece of card. The raised edges will form the outline when she rubs them. Be sure to cut out the centre of letters like 'O', 'B' and 'P'. You could make a face with button eyes and nose and cut out a cheesy grin, or a cat with slivers of paper for whiskers (the raised part only needs to be slightly raised to make an outline when rubbed).

What will particularly delight her is that, even though she can't yet draw properly, she can produce beautiful, realistic pictures through rubbings.

Not just fun but

★ Needs little equipment.
★ A good time filler.
★ A good cause-and-effect game.
★ Encourages the child to work towards an end.
★ Helps pencil control.

Spot the difference

Three to five years

One of the basic skills children have to master before they can read is to be able to see the small differences in shape between different words. At first children combine this skill with a bit of guess work to 'read words'. Because they get so much reward for this they look harder and develop this 'look and say' skill further. For most children the spelling out of words happens later. Any activity which encourages children to examine fine detail helps in the initial 'look and say' skill.

Draw a simple picture with clear strong lines – or trace one from a colouring book – and then trace this picture, making one detail different from the original. Ask her to spot the difference between the two pictures.

Not just fun but

★ Observational skills.
★ Essential practice of a pre-reading skill.
★ Matching skills – which underlie many mathematical ideas.
★ A visual memory skill – she has to remember what was in one picture while looking at the other.

With letters
She doesn't have to know the alphabet. Draw two lines of large, bold letters, with six or seven letters in each line. Change one letter in the second line and see if she can identify which. She won't know what the letters mean, but becoming familiar with them is important at this stage.

At the beginning try to make the difference quite obvious; if for example you've drawn a clown's face, you could give him a nose in one picture and no nose in the other one. You could give him hair in one picture and make him bald in the other.

This game is quite hard, and what seems obvious to you will not always be obvious to the child.

Later
Gradually make the differences more difficult to spot. Give the clown a smile in one picture and a sad, down-turned mouth in the other, or a small nose in one and a large nose in the other. Eventually you can draw pictures with two, then three, four and more differences.

Sound effects

Three to five years

Hearing is instinctive, paying attention to little sounds is not. In order to read children match the little sounds that make up words to letter shapes. This means that they have to learn how to pay attention to those little sounds.

It is easy to encourage your child to pay attention to sounds by pointing them out to him and helping him to find the language to describe them.

Not just fun but

★ Encourages careful listening. A vital skill for a child to master before he can read.

Also a skill for a child to master before he starts to learn music.

★ Encourages the child to pause before he acts.

With more than one child, turn the game into a small competition and see who can guess the source of the noise first.

For this game, you will need to gather together your props in advance and hide them under a cloth or towel. Stand behind a curtain, or behind his back; if he will tolerate a blindfold put one loosely over his eyes and then make numerous noises with your props. He has to guess what is making the noise. You could for instance jangle some keys, tear paper, crack a nut, close a door, knock on wood, switch on a light, ping elastic, play a note on a recorder or tin whistle, scrumple up paper, shut a book, rub a balloon, shake a rattle. If he can't guess, make the noise again once or twice, then give him a clue. If he still can't guess, tell him, and include that sound in the game the next time you play.

When he's ready, you can try sounds that are more difficult to distinguish: brushing hair, scratching material, shuffling cards.

Treasure hunt

Three years on

Treasures comes in all shapes and sizes but even the most humdrum objects can take on the greatest importance if they are included in this game. The game can be played by one child alone or by a whole roomful.

This is green and grows on trees.

This is found in the corner of envelopes.

You need this bag to make a cup of tea.

Clothes are made of

You will need this to travel on a train.

You are left with when you finish

Your basic equipment is a pencil, paper and some glue (see page 48). On a piece of paper draw a grid of squares, each of them roughly two inches by two inches. Inside each of the squares write a description of the 'treasure' needed to fill it. As each piece of treasure is found, glue it on to the right square.

You can vary the number of squares according to the age of the child and the length of time you want the game to last. The treasure needn't be complicated: a small button, a tea bag, a leaf, a blade of grass, a piece of material, a few grains of rice, a piece of pasta, a bus ticket or a shop receipt can all provide enough of a challenge.

For younger children you can include some squares that simply need to be coloured in with the right colour. For older children you can make the required objects more difficult to find.

As well as being great fun, this
game can also be played
competitively or co-operatively:
several children can work
together to complete one game or
they can race each other to
complete their own list.

ky and you
uts.

ip your drinks
gh this.

This clips papers together.

**Not
just fun
but**

★ Encourages the
child to use memory
and observation
skills.
★ Each square
presents a
different
challenge so the
game will often keep
the attention of even
the most easily bored
child.

That's silly

Three to five years

Children do not really understand jokes until they are about six – but that does not stop them enjoying silly and incongruous things. This language game will make your child think about word combinations, as well as allowing his imagination free rein. Its other great advantage is that you can play it anywhere – on car, bus, train or plane journeys, in a doctor's waiting room or, if you feel like a quiet time, at home.

Be ready to laugh even if they say the hen sat on the mat! Understanding silliness is much more complicated that it seems at first sight.

Not just fun but

★ Turn taking.
★ Social fun.
★ Helps language development.
★ Development of humour.
★ Thinking of two very different ideas to put together in one sentence helps the child to expand his attention span.

The idea is to make up and say a nonsensical sentence, like, 'We went to the playground on a flying carpet', or 'At the supermarket I bought a football stadium', or 'I go to bed wearing flippers'. He should reply, 'That's silly', and invent a silly sentence of his own. He will probably copy you, and tell you how he went to the playground, what he bought at the supermarket, or wore to bed.

Taking turns, which is an important aspect of the game, forms a valuable foundation for social interaction and basic conversation. Most important of all however is that he should perceive language as fun and laughter-provoking.

Some children – particularly older ones – find it hard to invent a silly sentence at all. One way to encourage them is to ask them to think of two completely different events: 'The cat sat on the mat' and 'The hen laid six eggs' and then combine the two – 'The cat laid six eggs'.

Making a camp

Three to five years

Not just fun but

W hen most of us look back on our childhood this is one of the games we remember.
If you have space in your garden, to put up a tent, this will be the answer. If not, or it's the depths of winter, help him to make a camp indoors. Look out a blanket, sheet, bedspread, old curtain or large tablecloth and drape it over a table or a piece of cord stretched between two solid chairs. Fix the material to the cord with clothes' pegs and weigh down the chairs with sacks of potatoes or heavy books. Provide your camper with a torch, sleeping bag and some cooking utensils.

★ Developing story telling skills enhance memory and planning.
★ Small spaces feel secure.
★ Pretending to be someone else helps him understand the idea of self and other.
★ Demands plenty of explanation and communication between children.

As children grow up you can emphasize their need for secrecy and the creation of a separate world with a sign written in invisible ink (lemon juice), a password and a book about codes.

Equip him with a rucksack, a pair of boots and 'a fishing rod' (a piece of string attached to a stick), and dispatch him to catch tea. He could cook his catch in a small frying pan on a wire rack resting on two shoeboxes. At teatime, why not give him a picnic in his tent? When he's older, you might even let him spend the night there. His excitement should dispel any feelings of discomfort.

Edible faces

Three years on

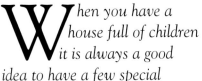

When you have a house full of children it is always a good idea to have a few special treats up your sleeve. Left to their own devices a gang of small children may egg each other on to naughtiness, or quarrel and fight over toys. This game is rather special because all the mess can be eaten and the 'naughty' behaviour – eating the 'sweet'– is perfectly harmless and part of the fun. The faces are made with chocolates and sweets.

Dress him in an apron and sit him at a table with a piece of rice paper, approximately the same size as a sheet of A4. Provide him with several small dishes filled with Smarties, small marshmallows, chocolate buttons, hundreds and thousands, chocolate chips and edible silver balls. Put out a bowl of melted chocolate, which will be sticky enough to act like glue, and a couple containing icing sugar and water mixture in different colours (use food colourings).

With a new paint brush or pastry brush, help him to paint a circle with the melted chocolate on the rice paper. This is the shape of the face. For the eyes, tell him to put two blobs of melted chocolate in the circle and stick smarties on top of them. Another chocolate blob and a marshmallow could be the nose. Give the face a red icing sugar and water paste mouth and pink cheeks.

Sprinkle hundreds and thousands or chocolate chips on top to give him some hair. A bow tie could be studded with silver balls, or if it's a female face, she could wear a necklace. When he has finished his face, don't forget to admire it before he sinks his teeth into it. If you are worried about sugar give them all a little toothpaste on a rag and suggest a bout of tooth cleaning.

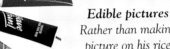

Edible pictures

Rather than making a face, he could paint a picture on his rice paper. Make a green icing sugar and water paste for grass and trees. You could use the melted chocolate for the trunks. You could buy tubes of ready-made piping (used for decorating cakes) to make his pictures or faces look more professional.

Not just fun but

★ A creative skill that can tempt the child who normally hates sticking and glueing.
★ Hand-eye co-ordination.
★ Brushing on chocolate uses the same skills as holding a pencil or brush.
★ A fun variation of craft skills which will appeal to all children.
★ A chance to be acceptably naughty by eating the materials.

Marbling paper

Three years on

This activity requires very little skill and yet the results can be stunning so, as long as you are are around to supervise, it's a perfect way to keep a three-year-old busy and happy. The aim is to create a version of the marbled paper that the Florentines make so beautifully and use to cover books, albums, boxes and frames, and which was fashionable in the 18thC for endpapers in books.

Not just fun but

★ Child has to follow instructions carefully.
★ Self expression through a creative activity.
★ Encourages the child to sit still and concentrate.
★ Good for hand-eye co-ordination.
★ The results look very special.

For this activity, you will need a shallow rectangular dish or roasting tin, which has to be larger than your sheets of paper. Start with white paper though later on you can create interesting effects by using different coloured paper, black in particular. Make enough home-made flour paste (see page 48) to fill the bottom of the dish. Squeeze approximately one tablespoonful of oil-based paint on to the surface of the paste. Use several different colours and swirl them into patterns with a lollipop stick.

Place a sheet of paper gently on top of the paint/paste mix, first making sure that there are no air bubbles on the surface. After 30 seconds or so, lift up the paper and lie it flat on a wire rack to dry. Use the same method for the other sheets of paper, but if you want to, swirl the mixture again to make a different pattern. No two sheets of marbled paper will ever look exactly the same. Experiment with different coloured paints.

Practical, too
*You can emulate the
Florentines and cover
cardboard boxes or
books with your
marbled paper, or use
it as wrapping paper,
or to make bookmarks
or greetings cards.*

String and marble painting

Three years on

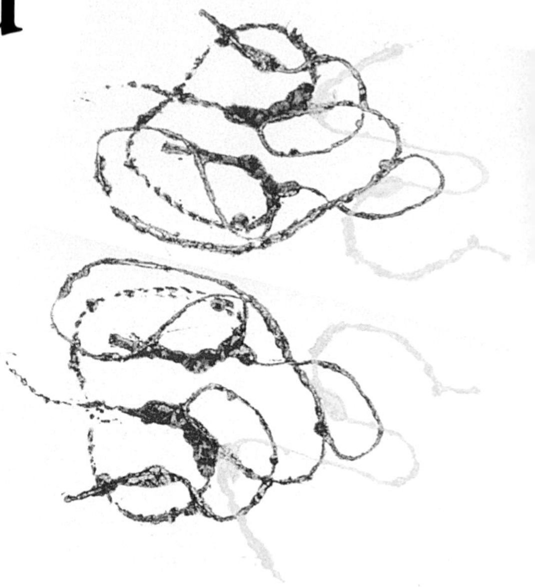

Once he has mastered finger, drip and blow painting (see page 44) and his finger control has improved, he could move on to these fun techniques. For string painting, set him up in the messy corner, in an overall, and give him several bowls of different coloured paint, some pieces of string and folded paper. Open up the paper, tell him to dip a piece of string in one of the bowls of paint leaving a few centimetres at the end dry, then show him how to place the string on the paper, making a curly pattern. Leave the dry end below the paper. Tell him to fold the paper in two, press down on it, and then carefully pull the string out. Encourage him to do the same with the other paint colours either before or after the first colour has dried. The effect will be quite different.

A cylinder – a biscuit tin for instance – will work for marble painting instead of a shoebox. You will have to roll up – and perhaps even cut – the paper to fit.

94

Marble painting

Painting with a marble is even simpler. Line a shoebox with a piece of paper, get him to dip a marble in paint, then put it in the box, fit the lid tightly and shake the box. He will love the noise it makes. He can take the marble out after a minute or so, wipe it and dip it into another colour and repeat the process. Do this with as many colours as you have. Finally take the paper out of the box and dry the picture flat.

Not just fun but

★ A nice cause-and-effect activity.
★ Good for the child who is often not satisfied with what he creates.
★ All forms of painting allow the child to work by himself.
★ Self expression through a creative activity.
★ Encourages the child to sit still and concentrate.
★ Good for hand-eye co-ordination.

Papier mâché

Three years on

Y ou and your child can make a host of
exciting things out of this versatile and
surprisingly durable material. Papier mâché
is inexpensive and easy to make, but it is messy, so
set up a 'messy' corner in your kitchen or playroom
and dress yourselves in aprons or overalls.

Without a mould
It is possible to model papier mâché
without using a mould, but make sure it is very thick.
It should have the consistency of clay, and you should be able
to work it in the same wqy. Papier mâché makes splendid
terrain – an island, a mountain or a farm, for example – and it
looks very impressive when you've painted it. Young children
may find it easier to mould using the inside of a bowl.

* Making the papier mâché is a social occasion.
* Making the models allows the child to work by herself.
* Self expression through a creative activity.
* Encourages the child to sit still and concentrate.
* Good for hand-eye co-ordination.
* A nice messy, feely activity for a small child.

Difficult shapes

It is sometimes easier to mould around a difficult shape if you start by building up the papier mâché from paper strips. Cut newspaper into strips and dip these into the paste. Leave until saturated with paste, then carefully take the strip and wrap it around the mould. Cover with a single layer then let this dry. Repeat with a second layer. You can continue it this way letting each layer dry before adding the next or switch to the papier mâché mixture. The dry paper surface acts as a better key.

Tear several days' worth of newspapers into strips about two by seven centimetres. Put the strips into a washing-up bowl of hot water for several hours until they are soft and breaking up. Squeeze all the water out of the newspaper, and mix it with homemade flour paste (see page 48) or PVA, watered down with three parts water to one part glue.

It can be used like clay. Another effective way to use papier mâché is to mould it around another object; for example, a plastic salt cellar or glass jam jar make excellent moulds for a pen holder. You can use an existing bowl as the mould for a papier mâché bowl, or for a mask. Cover your mould with Vaseline or cling film to make it easier to remove later.

To make an animal or a head, use a blown-up balloon, which you pop once the papier mâché is dry. To keep animals upright, sawn-off corks provide first-rate feet. Leave your object to dry for 24 hours, and if necessary give it another layer of papier mâché, and leave that to dry for a further 24 hours. When that layer is dry, she can paint the object with poster paints.

Collage

Three years on

Once your child has mastered 'snipping and sticking' (page 48), the natural development is making a collage. Save anything that might be useful: sweet papers, egg boxes, ribbon, string, wool, buttons, shells, feathers, leaves, wrapping paper, coloured felt, pieces of fabric, milk bottle tops, beads, sequins, tissue and crêpe paper, straws, doilies, and cotton wool. Different coloured, patterned and textured papers – smooth and matt, shiny, rough (sandpaper, for example) – will also be invaluable.

Night sky
A large piece of dark blue or black paper could be the basis for a night scene with silver foil stars.

More ideas

A collection of shells, some real sand, cocktail umbrellas and stripey material for towels and deck chairs makes a splendid beach scene. Include a few fish with silver foil or milk bottle top scales.

Egg boxes cut-up and painted green could be a terrifyingly fierce dragon. Make a stained-glass window from a mosaic of coloured tissue paper.

You will need a large piece of thick paper or card. Plan your picture before you start sticking. An outdoor scene is almost always a hit. You can introduce some elements from nature, using a piece of real bark for a tree trunk and a couple of feathers for a small bird, for example, and combine them with a bright yellow felt sun, tissue paper flowers and a silver foil pond. Tissue paper and cotton wool, which makes brilliant snowmen and snowflakes and can be painted to make fluffy animals, add a three-dimensional element to the collage. Beads and buttons are useful for eyes. People can be made more realistic with real fabric clothes, buttons and bows. Thick paper can be folded to form various objects. A concertina could be a fan or a staircase, for example. Use home-made paste (see page 48) or PVA.

Field hospital

Three years on

S mall children are often more caring and concerned about others than older children, perhaps because care-giving and -receiving are so essential to them at this stage. Like every other aspect of their lives, they like to play it through in games of pretence. Field hospital is typical of such games, but it has another purpose. Children fall and hurt themselves – they know only too well that accidents are possible. They also hear of other children who have been badly hurt, or have gone into hospital. A relaxed, happy game of hospitals, with all the blood and gore, but none of the pain, helps a child to come to terms with such fears: a way of dealing with worry and vulnerability.

Not just fun but

★ Makes them aware that care is not just something to receive, but to give.
★ Encourages thoughtfulness.
★ Helps confront and come to terms with fears.
★ Hand-eye co-ordination.

★ Planning: 'How do you get the bandage on?'
★ Language: 'Teddy needs some comforting words.'
★ Imagination and story-telling: 'How did Teddy hurt his head?'

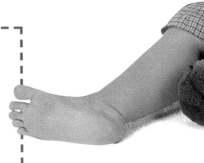

She will need a first-aid box or
plastic container, bandages or old
sheets torn into strips, cotton wool
or lint and plasters

Good impressions

Three years on

Young children vary enormously in their ability to handle a paint brush. Printing techniques allow children of all abilities to create attractive and interesting patterns quickly and easily. The simplest printing block is a potato. Slice one in half and gouge out a simple shape. The raised parts will print; the valleys will not. Rub this printing block in a saucer or pan of paint and then stamp on a sheet of paper.

Printing blocks can be made from all kinds of materials to create a range of interesting effects.

Printer's 'ink'
Use finger paint, starch paint (see page 45), or poster paint for printing. Place paper towels in the bottom of the paint dish to act as a stamping pad.

Cutting the stamps
Use a sharp kitchen knife. Keep the shapes as simple as possible. To add variety, give him three stamps, each with a different pattern.

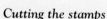

★ Understanding cause and effect: why things happen.

★ Precise placing of printing blocks improve hand and wrist skills.

★ Fine finger control: needed when helping to make the blocks.

★ Positioning the picture on paper improves the child's understanding of space. This type of spatial skill may well develop mathematical thinking.

★ Messy fun.

★ Understanding colour.

★ Understanding how things can be placed in a sequence, such as dark-to-light prints. An important mathematical skill.

★ Self-esteem. Making gifts that are appreciated means praise and recognition for the child: she feels good about herself.

★ Feeling 'I can do that'.

Each application of paint will yield two or three prints. See if he notices the gradual change in the depth of colour with each subsequent print. And that each print is a mirror image.

Pasta jewels

Three years on

The magic of this activity is that your child will witness the transformation of something ordinary into something extraordinary. Picking up the small pieces of pasta and threading them on to a ribbon will exercise her fine motor skills.

Necklace

Pasta is not just for eating, nor is it just spaghetti. Bows, wheels, spirals and tubes are just a few of the shapes which, when painted in bright poster paints, make stunning jewellery. The simplest piece to make is a penne and macaroni necklace. First, make sure that the macaroni is too large to fit inside the penne. Then ask your child to take 15 pieces of penne and 14 pieces of macaroni out of their packets, and help her to paint them in bright colours, or gold and silver for a more sophisticated effect. Paint one side of each piece, let it dry, then paint the other side. This way, you won't smudge them or get paint on your fingers. For a really professional look, when the paint is dry, finish the pasta pieces with clear varnish. Let her thread the pasta on to some ribbon or wool, helping her to alternate between the penne and the macaroni. Cut the ribbon or wool 40 or 50 centimetres longer than the necklace, and tie it at the neck. If the necklace is a success, your child could make a bracelet to match. You could use coloured beads instead of macaroni.

★ The child works under instruction – just as she will have to do at school.

★ Self expression through a creative activity.

★ Encourages the child to sit still and concentrate.

★ Good for hand-eye co-ordination.

★ The results look good and make the child feel proud.

Jewellery box
A box in which to keep the pasta jewellery will appeal to your child whether it is hers or she is giving it away as a present. Paint or cover the box. Paint a number of bows or wheels and, when dry, glue them on to the box. You could cover the box almost entirely or you could have a few strategically placed pieces.

Brooch
Experiment with other combinations of pasta shapes. Glue a line of fusilli, a pattern of bows, or a cluster of wheels on to a card and pin to make a range of unusual brooches.

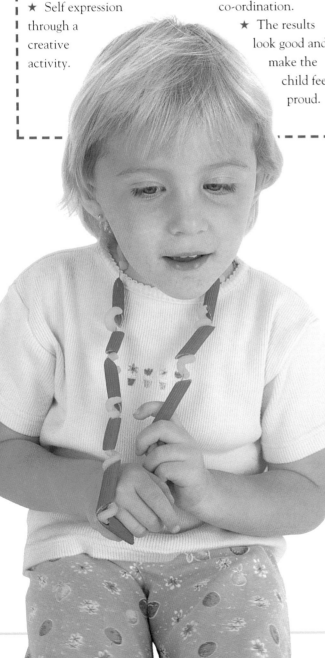

Open all hours

Three years on

Young children usually love playing at being grown-up and doing the jobs and activities they see their parents and other adults performing. Whereas real shopping can be a chore, a pretend shop provides an endless source of entertainment. Make a conscious effort to keep packets and cartons, egg-boxes and plastic bottles so that she has enough stock. Small unopened tins, mini cereal packets and samples will also come in handy. Write the prices on sticky labels. You might have some plastic fruit and vegetables, biscuits, cakes and loaves of bread; otherwise make them out of plasticine or papier mâché (see page 32).

You will need a low table (or a board resting on two large cardboard boxes) and ideally some shelves, on which to store the goods. Look out a set of weighing scales for the fruit and veg, which you could display in boxes with a scoop so that she can help herself. Make a till out of a shoe or an egg box, and give her some real money to add authenticity to the venture. Counting the money will be one of her first lessons in maths.

Talking shop

Encourage her to sort and arrange her stock. Ask her some simple arithmetical questions about how many tins of beans or packets of cereal she has in her shop. Go on frequent shopping trips. Sometimes bring something back and say you bought the wrong item and could you possibly change it? Sometimes she might like to let you run her shop and be the customer herself.

Not just fun but

★ A social game which encourages conversation.

★ Helps the child's memory. She must match her play to her knowledge.

★ Pretence encourages the child to think about herself and contrast this with her knowledge of others. Psychologists call this the development of a theory of mind.

★ The props of a pretend game help her to juggle ideas.

★ A sustained activity that can keep children amused for long periods.

★ Money and using scales can help with maths.

The advantage of a grocery store is that you can stock it easily with a variety of goods, but she can sell anything she likes in her shop: shoes, hats, clothes, cards (save old ones from Christmas and birthdays), books, toys or bread and cakes.

Noises off

Three years on

This game provides an effective way of calming down a group of children after they've been rampaging around the house or garden by making them concentrate on a story. Designed for a group of at least three children, it requires a small selection of musical instruments: a triangle or bell, a rattle or xylophone, a drum or two halves of a coconut shell.

Choose a story from a book. Perhaps one that they already know well like 'The Sleeping Beauty' and give each child a character, for whom he or she has to produce sound effects. The princess could be represented by the triangle or bell, the prince by the coconut halves or drum, and the wicked fairy by a rattle or xylophone. If there are more than three children, you could include other characters like the king and queen and the good fairies.

Gather the children around you and start reading the story. Every time one of the chosen characters is mentioned, the child with the appropriate instrument should play it. If you feel that the story in the book is too long, tell your own version. The advantage of doing this is that you can mention the characters' names more often.

Active, not passive
Children sometimes
become bored if you force
them to sit down and listen
to a story. This game
means that they are
actively participating in the
story, not just passively
listening. They will take
their roles very seriously
and wait with bated
breath for the next time
they have to produce
their particular
sound.

Not
just fun
but

★ A good social game.
★ A quiet party
game to intersperse
with other more
noisy
games.
★ Helps
children listen.
★ Good for the shy
child.

Making a noise appeals
to all children
whatever their age.
Noises off allows
them to make a noise
in a controlled, structured
way, and demonstrates how
sounds can enhance a story.

Suitable stories
Spend a little time considering which stories
will work best. Traditional fairy stories, like
Beauty and the Beast and Hansel and
Gretel, lend themselves to the game, but
you might also know some suitable modern
stories, or you can make up your own.

Little chef

Three to four years

Housework and cooking are only a chore because they have to be done. They are fun for children because it allows them to feel grown up – and they can eat the results. When you're busy cooking, it's easy to turf your child out of the kitchen and tell her to play somewhere else. Why not give her some simple tasks in the kitchen but out of your way? She could make up an instant powdered pudding: easy enough for a three-year-old to make on her own. Give her the correct amount of milk – all she has to do is add it and whip.

Not just fun but

★ Weighing and measuring help the child with mathematical ideas.

★ By the time they reach school children will need to know how to sit still, follow instructions and work until a task is completed. This is excellent practice for all of these skills.

★ Children like to feel useful.

★ Children need praise – and help with the chores invariably earns this.

★ Teaches children that families help each other.

Other tasks

Diluting squash; stirring a cake mix; greasing a cake tin; sieving flour; mashing potatoes; tearing off lettuce leaves; washing and drying a salad; squeezing oranges and lemons; rolling out pastry and cutting pastry shapes.

Later, let her help you make a cake. Find a basic recipe, read it out loud to her, and then allow her to weigh the ingredients, which will be a first maths lesson in itself. Then she can have fun mixing them all together. Best of all, when the cake has been baked, she can ice and decorate it.

Safety

Follow strict safety rules in the kitchen. Your child's cooking should always be supervised: a worthwhile tip is to have everything you need – ingredients and equipment – out and ready before you start. Make her wash her hands before she begins. Ensure she never gets her hands on sharp knives and keeps clear of electric food processors. Tell her to ask before tasting anything. Clear up spillages immediately. Don't let her take hot tins out of the oven or from under the grill or hot pans off the hob. Make sure no saucepan handles stick out.

When she has successfully prepared a dish, she could serve it in the 'Kids' café' (see page 136).

Magic painting

Three to five years

Your child will be both delighted and mystified by this painting game, which is derived from an Indonesian dyeing technique called batik. Without her knowledge, take an ordinary piece of white paper and draw a picture on it with the blunt end of a white wax candle. Then encourage her to paint the paper with watercolour and a thick brush. The paint will stick to the paper but not to the wax, so the previously invisible picture will magically begin to show. So that she understands how the magic painting is created, next time let her do the wax drawing as well as the painting. She could use a wax crayon instead of a candle.

★ Painting, writing and drawing all use very similar hand skills.

★ School work has a beginning, a middle and an end. Something that should be practiced before she gets to school. Complex techniques like this provides practice of doing things in sequence.

★ Painting the whole page teaches the child careful and thorough pen control.

★ Improves hand-eye co-ordination.

Stencils

Start her early on simple stencils, which you can make yourself from thick card, perhaps in a variety of shapes or animals, or even use paper doilies for an interesting effect. At first she can use wax crayons, then progress to colouring pencils and felt-tipped pens, before attempting paint. She might find it difficult to keep the stencil still, so you could tape a couple of edges to the paper with masking tape.

Scratch pictures

Making scratch pictures is another activity involving wax, but is much more difficult, so not really suitable for the under-fours. To do this, she must colour a thick sheet of paper with wax crayons (the denser the colouring the better), and then scratch out the outline of her picture with a plastic knife – or a blunt metal one. It might be easier for her to draw her

picture on top of the wax with a hard lead pencil first, before scratching it away. Beware, this activity is messy.

For a really elaborate scratching technique build up different layers of wax crayon starting with light colours and ending with dark blues and black. Then just scratch through to different depths.

Tracing

Three to five years

Tracing is an activity which most young children love. One reason for this is that, at a stage in her life when she can only produce a scribble if she draws free-hand, your child can trace a picture so that it looks almost exactly like the original. Although tracing obviously isn't as creative as free-hand drawing, it is excellent practice for pencil control and should be encouraged.

You'll need to buy some tracing paper and some white card the same size, or cut it to fit. On the card draw a simple drawing with bold lines. Look in her story and colouring books for inspiration if you're stuck for subject matter. If you don't feel up to doing the drawing yourself, you could always trace something and then tape the tracing paper on to the card. When she's ready to start tracing, pin her tracing paper on to the card with four paperclips, which will prevent the tracing paper from slipping. If it slips, it will be difficult for her to get it back in exactly the same place, and she will become frustrated.

Stained-glass effect
Buy some coloured tracing paper and when she has finished her tracing, stick it up on the window. It will look stunning with the light shining through it. Make a mosaic of different coloured papers to create a stained-glass effect.

In case of difficulty
Holding a pencil is the first skill a child needs – directing it comes close behind. Tracing takes it one stage further. It is difficult because the child needs good hand control. If your child finds tracing too frustrating – and many children do – make the shapes very simple. I always found the best way to start was to make lines of dots for them to practice with first.

Not just fun but

★ Child has to work towards an end.
★ Helps the child learn to sit still and concentrate.

★ Helps the child to develop pencil control.
★ Practice at following lines helps the child learn to write.

The baby clinic

Three to five years

Children play through their experiences in pretend games. A baby is a major life event and naturally generates lots of pretence – from breast feeding a teddy to bathing a doll. This is such a simple game that even a child with no experience soon picks up the rules. It is popular with both girls and boys in nursery schools.

To set up the clinic you will need a row of chairs for the waiting area and a low table where you can put a set of scales and a tape measure. The game is ideally played with several children. Two can be 'parents' who bring their 'baby', a doll or even a teddy, to the clinic for his three-month check-up. Another child can play 'doctor'. She will need a white coat – an old white shirt with the sleeves rolled up will do – and, if you have one, a toy doctor's bag, complete with stethoscope and syringe.

You could make a basic graph or chart for the baby's height and weight. If, when they return to the clinic for the next check-up, the parents bring in a larger doll or teddy, they could fill in the chart – with a little help from you – and see at a glance how much longer and heavier their baby has become.

Nappy-changing

Buy a small pack of the smallest size disposable nappies for the parents to bring into the clinic with them. More than anything else the children love changing the baby's nappy. The doctor can weigh and measure the baby, listen to his heart and give him his three-monthly injections. If there are more children involved in the game, they could also be parents, and one child could be the health visitor, whose role might be to advise on what food to give the baby and even help with a meal or a bottle.

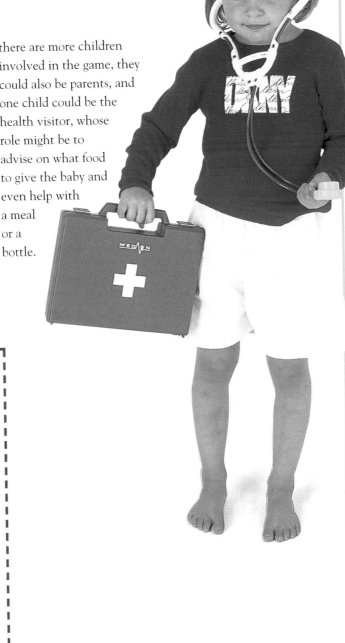

Not just fun but

★ Recreating past experience improves memory.

★ Telling a story helps a child to organize thoughts and experiences.

★ Explaining roles helps children understand the concept of self and other.

★ Helps the child realize that other people have different experiences.

★ Play with dolls and teddies always includes language.

★ Encourages the gentle caring side of the child's nature.

Pass the parcel

Three to five years

A traditional party game, 'pass the parcel' is an excellent way of encouraging children to share. It is only possible to play if there are three children or more, and you will need to have spent some time wrapping a parcel in layer after layer of paper, done up with sticky tape. Try not to use too much, as it makes it very difficult and time-consuming for small fingers to undo.

When playing with the youngest children I always put a tiny present (just a sweet or a tiny sticker) in each layer.

Stick to the rules
You will probably find that some children are reluctant to let the parcel go once they've unwrapped their layer, but insist that they stick to the rules of the game. Wrapped up like a birthday present and the contents a surprise, the parcel is the most sought-after toy in the world.

Make sure that every child receives a little present later. If they don't feel hard done by, they will learn the art of sharing through this game.

Not just fun but

★ A good party game.
★ A social game which encourages laughter.
★ Encourages the child to be unselfish.
★ Good for fine finger skills.

The children sit in a circle and start passing the parcel around from one to another while you play some lively music. Every now and then, stop the music and the child who is holding the parcel at that moment unwraps a layer of paper. The game continues and the turns become shorter, until the lucky child who unwraps the last layer of paper is allowed to keep the present inside. Stop the music at strategic moments to ensure that all the children have an opportunity to unwrap the parcel.

Simon says

Two to four years

An old favourite, 'Simon says' is a game for a group. The advantages are that it can be played almost anywhere and needs no special equipment. Start the game by being the leader yourself, and gather the children in a circle around you, either sitting or standing. Begin by calling out simple commands like, 'Simon says, put your hands on your head', and demonstrate the command yourself. The children must obey you. Continue with other commands such as, 'Simon says, put your hands on your knees', 'Simon says, cross your arms', 'Simon says, clap your hands', 'Simon says, sit down'. Every now and then say, 'Touch your toes' or 'Stand up', omitting the, 'Simon says'. Without the magic words, the children must not follow these commands.

Inevitably some will fall into the trap and if they do copy you, they should go out. Let all the children have a go at being Simon – or they might prefer to use their own names.

Not just fun but

★ Spatial skills. Movements must be copied.
★ Observation.
★ Social play.
★ Playing and laughing together forges friendships.

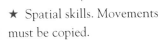

Through the arches

Three to five years

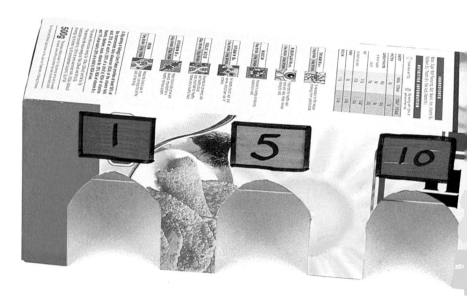

With toy cars
Marbles are probably the
easiest objects to roll straight
and he should soon master
the technique. However he
may prefer to play the game
with toy cars although they
have a tendency to turn
over, particularly on carpet.

For this game, you will need at least 10 marbles and a large cereal packet. By the age of three, a child will usually have stopped putting marbles in his mouth and his hand-eye co-ordination will be advanced enough to attempt shooting them at a target, which is the object of 'Through the arches'. Cut the cereal packet in half lengthways, so that you have a long, narrow five-sided box, and cut four arch shapes into one of the two long sides. Above each arch stick a label with

a number on it (1, 2, 3, 4, or 5, 10, 15, 20), which will signify the points gained when someone shoots a marble through that arch. Help him to position himself low on the floor – squatting or lying down – a couple of metres from the row of arches. Take it in turns to roll the marbles. Each time one goes through an arch, that person scores the number of points written above it. For a three-year-old, you could have a pot of counters beside you and give him the same number as his score, a ploy that will work wonders for his number recognition.

Not just fun but

★ Good for learning how to take aim.
★ Experience with simple adding.
★ Good for hand-eye co-ordination.
★ Sense of achievement boosts confidence.
★ A simple game which does not need much preparation.

Pairs

Three to five years

Small children often have better visual memories than adults so this is a game that can be played on equal (or almost equal) terms.

You will probably have a pack of picture cards, with which you and your child can play the game, traditionally called pelmanism. If not, you can make your own. One advantage of doing this is that you can choose what to draw on them. Make the pictures simple with bold, clear lines (the pictures on some bought cards are too busy), and for older children you can introduce subtle differences. Draw them on large pieces of card or ideally plain white postcards.

Numbered version

You can use this game to help him with numbers. On 20 cards, draw 10 pairs of beach balls from one to ten balls; the card with one ball on it has to be matched with another card with one ball on it, and so on. Or play traditional pelmanism with normal playing cards.

Random layout

An older child can cope with more pairs, no longer set out in rows, which makes the game so much easier for young children, but in an unstructured group.

Good ideas for pictures are straightforward household objects: a spoon, cup or plate; animals: a cat, duck or ladybird; vehicles: boat, car, bus or train; toys: ball, doll or teddy; or anything familiar to him from a house to a tree. If he's only three when you first play 'pairs', use 12 cards (six pairs) and lay them out in four rows of three. Turn over two cards at a time, keeping any that match to one side. At first play the game together and when he feels confident enough, take it in turns. Young children often have surprisingly accurate memories.

The older the child, the more cards you can include in the game. By the time he is six, you can introduce some cards which look like other cards but have subtle differences: one pair showing two cakes, another showing one; one pair of black cats, one of ginger cats; one pair of short-haired dolls, one of dolls with long plaits; one pair of ladybirds with six spots, another pair with four spots.

Pictures/words
Another variation is to have one picture card, which has to be matched with a word card, where its name is spelt out; so you have a picture of a cat and a card with c-a-t written on it.

Strategy
Children under six rarely use strategy. They go for the card they are most certain of first – then the one they feel unsure about. Those over six do the reverse – which can be a source of frustration when the older child takes what the younger one considers 'his' cards.

Buried treasure

Three to five years

Full-scale treasure hunts are great for family parties. But even if it's just you writing the clues and your four-year-old doing the hunting, few children can resist the challenge of looking for buried treasure, with its combination of mystery and anticipation. The treasure itself need not be anything more complicated than something to eat.

You must devise (and hide) a trail of clues with each clue suggesting where the next is to be found until at last the treasure is reached. For younger players who can't yet read you will need to draw clues rather than write them – just be careful not to overestimate your own artistic skills or your young detectives may have a hard time.

If you are entertaining children of all ages give the little ones the simple clues and the big ones much harder clues – or let the little ones find the right room and the big ones the right place (or vice versa).

Number of clues

Try not to make the trail too long (somewhere between five and ten clues is ample) and if you are drawing the clues, stick to fairly easily recognizable locations: the television, an armchair, under the stairs, a bookcase and so on. If the weather is fine and you have a garden don't forget to include one or two places outside. Then all you have to do is hand over the first clue and watch the fun.

CLUE

You will find in the garden next to the appl tree.

CL

You me i bedr the w

Not just fun but

★ A good party game or when children come to play.
★ Good for children of all ages – older children can play with a younger partner.
★ Simple reading practice.
★ Matching pictures with objects.
★ Memory and planning skills.
★ Exuberance, letting off steam.
★ Exercise.

CLUE

You will find me in the sitting room next to the sofa.

The post office

Three to five years

Children's early make believe games always involve things they know. This game, a variation on a make-believe shop (see page 106), incorporates some different elements and can be just as much fun. Keep jiffy bags that are sent to you, envelopes of all shapes and sizes, junk mail, postcards, and brown paper. Stuff newspaper into the jiffy bags and wrap a few shoe boxes in brown paper to make parcels. Stick labels over old envelopes, write new addresses on them and remove the old stamps. Get your child to make her own stamps out of sticky coloured paper or labels. Choose different colours for first class and second class.

You don't need an expensive toy post office kit to play this game. All the props are things that you will have around the house or can be put together in a few minutes.

Not just fun but

★ A social game which encourages conversation.
★ Helps the child's memory. He must match his play to his knowledge.
★ Pretence encourages the child to think about himself and contrast this with his knowledge of others. Psychologists call this the development of a theory of mind.
★ The props of a pretend game help him to juggle ideas.
★ A sustained activity that can keep children amused for long periods.

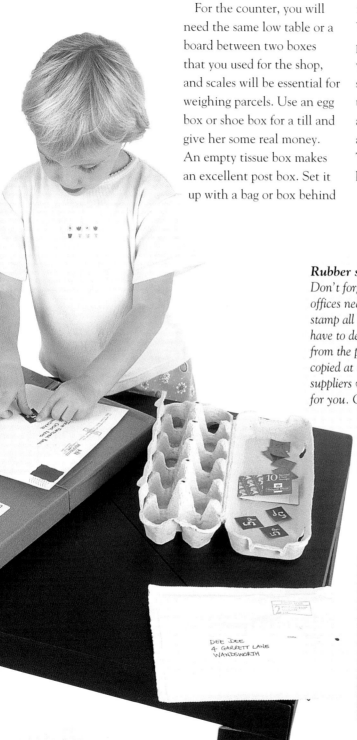

For the counter, you will need the same low table or a board between two boxes that you used for the shop, and scales will be essential for weighing parcels. Use an egg box or shoe box for a till and give her some real money. An empty tissue box makes an excellent post box. Set it up with a bag or box behind it for the letters to drop into. When she is in charge of the post office, she can weigh your mail, sell you stamps, stick them on for you, collect the letters from the post box, and even distribute them to all her toys around the house. Take turns and sometimes let her play the role of customer.

Rubber stamp

Don't forget the rubber stamp. All offices need one. She will need one to stamp all those forms post office staff have to deal with. (Pick up the forms from the post office and get them copied at the copy shop). Office suppliers will make up a rubber stamp for you. One with their names, and one with the date were my children's all-time favourite stocking filler!

Paying up

With an older child, you can write the value on the stamps, making them in different colours to denote their different values. Help her to add up how much your stamps will cost and to sort out the right change. Keep the maths simple.

Pressing flowers

Three years on

With all the environmental pressure on wild flowers, it is probably advisable to leave all but the most common where you find them growing and enjoy them there. Garden and commercially grown flowers can be pressed just as successfully. The best flowers for pressing have small delicate petals – buttercups and snowdrops, pansies and sweetpeas. The petals of flowers like roses and peonies are too fleshy, but can be pressed separately and used in a collage (see page 98).

Before you start pressing, examine the flower closely with your child. Point out the various elements that make it up: the stem, petals, leaves, buds, stamens, seeds and carpels.

You don't need to buy a flower press; simply place the flower carefully between two pieces of blotting paper, or tissue paper, and then put it between the pages of a heavy book. Close it and place two or three more large books on top. Leave your flower to press for a month or so. Try and resist the temptation to keep looking to see how it's coming along.

Displaying and using

When it is pressed, you could use the flower to make a greetings card or a bookmark. All you will need is some good-quality card and clear sticky-backed plastic. Alternatively, cut the card to fit a small photograph frame and make a framed picture (the glass should keep the flower in place without having to stick it down), a present which he'll be proud to give since he helped to make it himself.

★ Sustained activity.
★ Teaches the child to plan.
★ Teaches the child to work by herself.

★ Teaches the child to sit still and concentrate.
★ Many of the collecting tasks involve hand-eye co-ordination.
★ Helps categorization.
★ Teaches the child about nature.

Try choosing different coloured card for the background to make the colour of the flower stand out.

Talking point
Ask him about how the pressed flower looks different from the fresh flower. How has the colour changed?

Map making

Three years on

Children under seven have a very poor idea of how things are connected in space. A small child will not be able to make a complex map but she can make a very simple one, as described below.

You will need a large sheet of paper and a supply of pencils, crayons or felt-tipped pens and, if you have them, little wooden or plastic trees and houses, and toy cars. Take a simple journey – just one or two streets no more and make a map to represent it. Start with your own street; put in your house and your neighbours' plus landmarks like the post box, church, bridges, bus stops or schools.

If you have them, include some model trees and houses. You could even make the special and interesting buildings yourself. When you have finished the map, make the journey in a toy car. Discuss what you see on the way. You could fill the roads with cars, buses, taxis, police cars and even road works (see page 56).

Not just fun but

★ Encourages spatial skills.
★ Encourages observation.
★ Fine finger skills.
★ Working towards an end.
★ Encourages the child to sit still.

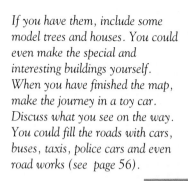

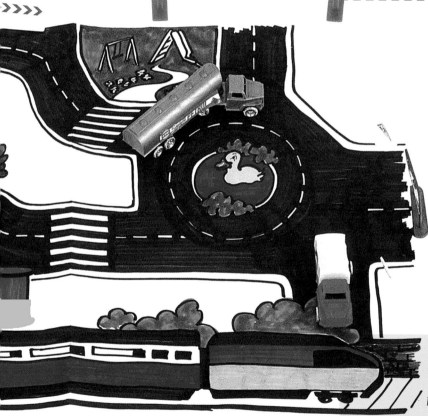

If she finds this task too difficult, start by taking a series of photographs (or make drawings) of landmarks along a well-trodden route. Now help her arrange these in order. Once she can do this draw out the road and let her arrange them. She will gradually get the idea.

Blind tasting

Three years on

Taste is perhaps the most neglected of the senses to be explored in children's games. At two, they are still developing their individual sense of taste and can change their minds from one week to the next about what they will and won't eat. Some children of this age are extremely fussy and will only eat a few types of food. Through playing this fun guessing game, your child will encounter some new flavours without realizing it. She might even start experimenting with more varied foods herself.

Not just fun but

★ A challenging game which explores senses we do not usually use in isolation.

★ A social game which is less about winning and more about laughing.

★ Encourages the child who is self conscious to cope with getting things wrong.

★ Versions of this game can get exuberant without becoming too wild.

Older children have a more developed sense of taste, so you can adapt this game to make it more difficult for them. Use different coloured wine gums, for example, and see if they can detect which one is which.

Blind touching

You could also adapt the game to explore the sense of touch. For drinks and plates of food, substitute toys (a plastic figure, a piece from a jigsaw, a toy bus), or anything you have around the house from a whisk to an orange or a shell. See if your child can tell what the object is by its feel.

Fill four or five beakers with different drinks, such as Ribena, apple juice, orange juice, lemon squash and water. Prepare four or five bowls of fruit or vegetables. Most children like grapes, kiwi fruit, apple, banana and cucumber, for example. Then place four or five different biscuits on plates. Use whatever you find in your biscuit tin and include some savoury ones, like water biscuits or oatcakes, and some sweet ones – jammy dodgers, custard creams, ginger or chocolate biscuits. Put a soft cloth blindfold over her eyes and help her taste the various drinks. See if she can identify them. To make it easier, you could give her the four or five possibilities. Do the same with the food.

Eyeful

I used to play the version of this game which involved feeling things we could not see (see top of page). It was called Nelson's lost body parts. The best bit (or the worst depending on how you look at it) was feeling for his eye. This was usually a slug but I remember that a boy at school once had a real eye that he got from his uncle who was a butcher. We all screamed when he got it out of his pocket and nobody could touch it.

Paper plate faces

Three to five years

A supply of paper plates will be invaluable in your store cupboard since they can be used for a range of craft activities. This one transforms them into pictures that can be hung on playroom walls, masks for dressing up or play clocks.

To make a clown face, cut out a circle of bright red sticky paper (or use a round red sticker) and ask your child to stick it in the middle of a paper plate. Make a fringe from orange wool or paper, and glue it to the top of the plate for his hair. He could draw crosses with a black felt-tip for the eyes and make a big smile out of the red sticky paper. If you make holes through the centre of the eyes and two more holes at each side of the face, through which you thread a piece of elastic, you will have a clown mask.

Give your paper plate face a thatch of cotton wool hair, a cotton wool beard, black beady eyes, a red felt hat and jolly red cheeks, and he will be Father Christmas.

A paper plate is also the perfect basis for a clock face. Help him to write the numbers from one to 12 evenly spaced around the edge of the plate. It's easier if he writes 12, six, three and nine first. Cut two strips of card – one slightly longer than the other – to represent the hands and fix them on to the plate with a paper fastener.

Remember the clock goes around twice in a day. This can be quite confusing for the child. Make this clear by having a double rim. Fill in midnight to midday on one circle and midday to midnight on the other. Put the symbols on each circle.

Keeping time

Before you pin on the hands, your child could decorate the clock face with a picture or series of pictures. Perhaps he could draw things that would remind him of what happens at various times throughout the day; for instance, a plate of sausages, potatoes and peas at 12 or one, a cake at four, a bed at seven, moon and stars at ten, a sun at six and a bowl of breakfast cereal at eight.

Not just fun but

★ Fine finger skills.
★ Working towards an end.
★ Encourages the child to sit still.
★ Introduces the child to a clock face.

Bird pudding

Three to five years

Making a pudding for the birds is one of the best kitchen games and an ideal way to occupy a child on her own on a rainy afternoon. Provide her with large quantities of suitable seed, grated suet, scraps of meat, breadcrumbs, nuts and dried fruit. When she has mixed these ingredients together in a bowl YOU add melted lard to bind the mix. The lard has to be kneaded in thoroughly – a delightfully messy business which she's sure to enjoy. Once she has done this, push a piece of knotted string well into the mix and then mould it into an old yoghurt pot and leave to harden. When it is hard, turn the pudding out of the pot and hang it ouside for the birds. It will be very satisfying for the child to see the birds flock to enjoy the fruits of her labour.

Robin

Swallow

Greenfinch

See if you can recognize any regular visitors to your bird table. Use a bird book, such as **The Shell Easy Bird Guide**, ideal for kids.

Waxwing

Song thrush

Not just fun but

Redwing

★ Helps the child to work towards an end.
★ Requires the child to pay attention and watch carefully.
★ Helps the child to understand that things must be done in the right order.
★ A quiet activity.
★ Doing things together encourages conversation.
★ Teaches the child to follow instructions.
★ A caring activity.
★ Encourages her to learn bird names.

Mistle thrush

Whitethroat

Kids' café

Three to five years

Playing through an experience is a way of thinking about what happened. Small children have quite a short memory span so organizing their thoughts is quite difficult unless they have an adult to jog their memory or props to remind them. A meal or a drink in a café is a common treat but unless he eats out regularly a three year old will probably need an adult or older sibling to remind him of most of the details. Cafés can be quite simple – just a table and a chair with a pretend hamburger or something altogether more elaborate. Because three- to four-year-olds play what they know, there is no point introducing a waiter if he only ever eats at a burger bar. Of course, he can learn a more elaborate game at playschool.

You and your child could make attractive centrepieces from painted toilet rolls filled with pipe cleaner and paper flowers. If you don't have enough small chairs, use buckets or wastepaper bins turned upside down. Encourage him to decorate pretty patterns on place mats out of coloured card, and make a menu together. You write the name of each dish; he can illustrate it.

Lay the table with toy or paper plates, plastic cutlery and paper napkins. Use a mixture of real, plastic and play dough food.

Bill, please
The waiter must bring the bill at the end of the meal. He hopes his customers have enjoyed it and that there won't be any disputes. Have a cash box or till for the money or 'cheques'.

Being a customer is a bit dull so collect an assortment of teddies and soft toys to be your customers. The main characters are the waiter and the one person giving the order. You can play one role – or he can play both. One of you can be the waiter, the other the chef. The waiter should escort the customers to their seats, hand out the menus and take down the orders. If he can't write, give him a pad and pencil anyway; he can pretend with a few scribbles. If you need another role, the chef can always be slaving over a hot cardboard stove, creating play dough delicacies.

Not just fun but

★ Remembering events into the right sequence is easier if he has the props to remind him what comes next.

★ Recreating an experience helps children tell a story.

★ Pretend play helps children understand that other people have separate thoughts and feelings.

★ When children play through their experiences they stretch their memory capacity.

★ If children share the experience they can also share the game. Two memories are better than one, together they may be able to remember everything that happened. It is just one of the advantages of having a sibling.

Jam jar symphony

Three to five years

E ven adults are fascinated by the musical effects of tapping a spoon on a glass of water. Young children, who are less demanding about the need for 'real' tunes, enjoy it even more.

Find 10 or 12 glass bottles or jars. Milk bottles or jam jars are ideal, but wine, beer or sauce bottles will do. If necessary, use a funnel to pour the water inside. Also find a selection of drumsticks: paint brushes, chopsticks or wooden spoons are practical; you could try a metal spoon, too.

Ask the child to pour the water into the bottles, making sure that none are full and that they contain different amounts of water for different notes. Then it's over to the child: he or she will soon start to experiment with different bottles to produce different notes in different order.

★ How to work things out.
★ How to do things for oneself.
★ Can be messy – and therefore fun.
★ Listening carefully.
★ How to fit things into sequences, for example, low to high notes.
★ Basics of music-making.

Provide a jug for pouring water and a large plastic bowl to receive excess water from the bottles; this excess could also replenish the filler jug. It is wise to play the game on the floor or on a low table to minimize breakages.

If playing the game outdoors, where stains are less of a problem, you could add different food colourings to the bottles. The child might then colour-code his or her tunes.

Boxed in

Four years on

How often have you noticed that the box a toy came in gets more attention than the toy itself? Cardboard boxes usually top the popularity poll. With a selection of these boxes, strong sticky tape, PVA glue and paint a child can make anything from a steam-engine to a spaceship. Get him to suspend his disbelief by making up a tale of high adventure to suit the vehicle under construction. In no time he'll be soaring through the Milky Way.

As children get older their games become more elaborate, but the best game is often the simplest. For every box that gets turned into *a* spaceship there are a least half a dozen left as they were found at the supermarket. In each one you are likely to find a very contented toddler just sitting happily.

Making a castle needs imagination, ingenuity and manual skill. Assembling the armour and planning the attack needs an enthusiastic flow of good ideas and starts to develop a spirit of co-operation amongst the rescue team – and flattening the castle at the end is not only heaps of fun but also makes it easier to fit into your re-cycling box or dustbin.

Castle Doom

For a group of children an old-fashioned castle presents countless possibilities. Make the grim keep of Castle Doom the prison where the wicked king has locked up the beautiful princess (or handsome prince). The castle has to be built, armour and appropriate weapons procured, and plans laid for the successful siege and rescue of the prisoner. Then, best of all, comes the razing of the evil castle to the ground. Remember to give each child a part to play so that they can all pride themselves on the successful outcome.

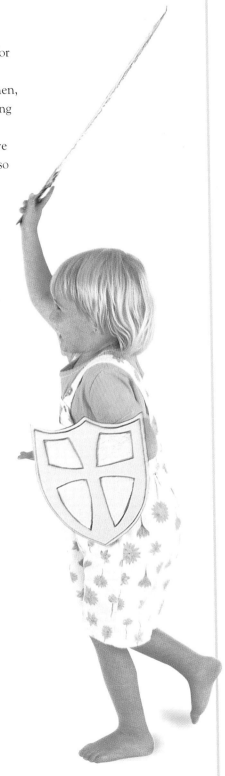

Not just fun but

* ★ Encourages the child to play with others.
* ★ Pretend games help the child to remember stories.
* ★ Pretend games encourage the child to think about the contrast between themself and others.
* ★ Teaches the child to work towards an end.
* ★ Good for hand-eye co-ordination.
* ★ A good way to keep a small child amused when you are busy.
* ★ Sense of achievement boosts confidence.

Duck, duck, goose

Four to five years

This structured version of tag can be played indoors. It is a game for at least four or five children – preferably more. Seat the group in a circle on chairs or the floor. Select one child to be 'it'. She must walk around the outside of the circle, tapping each child she passes, saying, 'duck'. Without warning, when she feels inclined, she should suddenly say, 'goose' to one of the children.

Making it fair
Keep an eye out to make sure that a younger, slower child doesn't find herself stuck as 'it'. You could introduce a rule that no child remains 'it' for more than three goes, and take it upon yourself to appoint a new one.

Not just fun but

★ Lets off steam – which all children need every day.
★ The stop-go nature of tag games provides exactly the right pattern of activity for optimal development of muscle and bone.
★ Social game which involves both competition and trust.

At this, the 'goose' jumps up and chases 'it' around the circle, trying to catch her before she reaches the empty seat or space in the circle. If 'it' succeeds in giving 'goose' the slip and reaches the empty seat before being caught, 'goose' becomes 'it' and the game starts afresh. If, on the other hand, 'goose' catches 'it', the same child remains as 'it' – at least – for the next round.

Most party games involve exuberance, noise and excitement. Something which is inevitable once a gang of children get together. Remember excitement can so easily lead to tears. Especially as small children approach bedtime.

Pipe-cleaner characters

Four to six years

O nce she has made her cardboard village (see page 56) or a papier mâché scene (see page 96), or turned a cardboard box into a simple dollshouse, she will need to people them with some little figures. Pipe cleaners come in a variety of different colours and can be twisted together to make miniature men, women, children, animals, trees and cars. Even if she doesn't have a scene to fill, she could make the characters and invent a story around them. This could focus on a trip to the circus, a visit to the zoo or, if she finds people easier to make than animals, a shopping expedition or a holiday. The story will give the game a structure, and give her ideas about which figures to construct.

Straws can be used instead of pipe cleaners to construct model people, animals and objects. The best kind to use are the ones with a bendy section about a third of the way down the straw.

Pipe cleaners pre-date construction toys, but are splendid, even more versatile substitutes. Making models from them will not only improve her manipulative skills but will also teach her about shape. She will have to consider carefully the shape of every model she makes – people, animals and objects.

Assistance
You will need to help younger children but they will soon get the hang of folding over one pipe cleaner to make the head, body and legs and wrapping a smaller section of pipe cleaner around to make the arms. Cut the pipe cleaners up for the child as this is rather difficult to do.

Not just fun but

★ Excellent practice for fine finger movements.
★ The child has to plan this activity and follow the rules.
★ 'Little worlds' help the child understand the social interactions he observes in the world around him.
★ A family of stick people can live through (and survive) the things that frighten him. This is an excellent way of dealing with his worries. Playing happily with something that in reality frightens him is the best psychotherapy.

Green fingers

Four years on

Using sunlight and water to turn a dull looking seed into a living, growing plant is a source of endless pleasure to a child. Through three simple experiments, you can show him what plants need in order to develop.

A plant needs light

Dampen two small sponges or two handfuls of potting compost (even sawdust will do) and put them on to separate saucers. Scatter some grass seed over each saucer and put them somewhere warm and light, covering each with a glass bowl. Both will soon start to send up green shoots. Change one of the bowls for a china or tin one – and show her how the shoots underneath this bowl eventually turn pale and die.

A plant needs water

One morning fill a jam jar with water and add some bright food colouring. Cut off the bottom of a stick of celery or a carrot and get her to stand it right way up in the jar. Towards the end of the day take out the vegetable and cut it into shorter lengths to see how far up it has taken the coloured water.

Roots and shoots

Put some mung beans in the bottom of a jam jar and cover them with a pad of damp cotton wool or kitchen paper. In a week or so the beans will have spread their roots round the bottom of the jar and will be starting to send shoots up through their covering.

Minature garden
Start with a thin layer of soil on a tray or a plate. Use a little mirror or the shiny side of a piece of kitchen foil to make a pond. Add moss, stones, twigs and a few small plants to make a wonderful display.

Not just fun but

★ Simple science gives factual knowledge.
★ Encourages the child to experiment.
★ Helps the child to develop logical thought.
★ Teaches the child to work towards an end.
★ Teaches the child to work by himself.
★ Teaches the child to concentrate.
★ Elements of the tasks are good for hand-eye co-ordination.
★ Sense of achievement boosts confidence.

Water...
If she wants to progress beyond the simple experimental stage and, because failures are such a disappointment, get a book on the subject, both as a source of more ideas and to learn how to produce a wide variety of healthy, thriving plants.

Which comes first?

Four years on

Children under four find sequencing difficult – and even after four. Here is a game that will help. Look out some family photographs – children love them. You can show sequences of a journey, the seasons, a meal being eaten or something rather more difficult like growing older.

By now the child will understand that there is a continuation between birth and death and that people are themselves throughout. This idea is quite new to them and so of special interest. Find some photos of yourself or one of her grandparents when young. You need four photographs in sequence: as a baby, small child, young adult and a recent one of the person as he or she is now. Muddle the photos up and ask her to sort them into order.

Chicken and egg

You can also play this game with drawings on cards. Draw an egg, the egg cracking and chicken hatching, a fluffy chicken and a full-grown hen, or a seed in the ground, a small seedling, a larger seedling with roots and a flower. If she is younger than four, you could make the sequence simpler, and have three pictures of a plate full of food, one that is half empty and one that is completely empty. If she is older, make the sequences more complicated. Draw scenes from a typical day: breakfast, school, lunch, tea, bathtime, bedtime, sunset or cut up frames from a simple comic strip.

Not just fun but

★ A challenging game which encourages the child to understand the sequences of events.
★ Helps the child to understand about the continuity of self.
★ Helps the child to understand about self and other.
★ Helps the child put things in order.
★ Helps the child to understand the passing of time.

Memory tray

Four years on

Three and four year olds cannot play games which involve strategy – so we always have to make allowances for them – and this makes the games dull. Because three to six year olds often have exceptional 'photographic' memories games like memory tray and pairs (page 120) can often be played on equal terms with older children and adults.

You can play the game with one child on his own, or make a party game of it if you have a group. Choose a few well-known or easily recognized objects; not too many to start with, as he and his friends will be overwhelmed by having to remember them all.

The first time you play, put five or six objects – perhaps a cup or beaker, a small toy, a piece of fruit, a book, a pen, a rubber ball – on a tray. Allow him to see the tray for about 30 seconds and then cover it with a cloth or towel. See how many of the objects he can remember. If he has difficulty, you can always give him clues. With a group, you could give each one a felt tip pen and a piece of paper and ask them to draw the objects they remember. The one who remembers the most is the winner.

★ Encourages careful observation.
★ Good visual memory task.
★ A game a small child can win.
★ Good family fun.

With older children

The more often you play the game, the more objects you can introduce. If you're playing with older children, you might have at least ten objects and some quite difficult ones like a pair of scissors, cotton reel, shell, coin, stamp, old tube or theatre ticket and playing card.

Once children start school, they will need to rely on their memories more and more. They will not only have to remember facts and concepts, but also their possessions. Memory games will help them to start taking on this responsibility for themselves.

Making lists

Children of seven years and older can write down the names of the objects they remember on the tray. Children of four can draw them as long as they have clear, simple lines – like a banana or an apple, a ball, a cup or a toy car.

Noughts and crosses

Four years on

By four, your child may be ready to take on a noughts and crosses challenge. Fitting circles and crosses in boxes may be too difficult for him, so play the game on a home-made board, made up of nine squares, and mark ten cards, five with noughts and five with crosses. Playing in this way makes it easier for a child to spot a completed line. Explain the rules of the game simply. Show him that first he places a cross on one of the squares and then you place a nought on another one, and that you carry on taking turns like this until one of you wins by completing a vertical, horizontal or diagonal line. The concept of turn-taking in games is essential for him to learn.

Not just fun but

★ A game that small children are good at.
★ Teaches the child about winning and loosing.
★ A social game, one of the few that can be played by children of different ages.

It is unlikely that he will understand tactics at four, or even that he must try to prevent you from winning as well as trying to win himself. But it is surprising how, with practice, even a four-year-old can start beating his parents. It might be a good idea to let him win sometimes, just to boost his morale.

One of the great advantages of noughts and crosses is that it can be played almost anywhere – from a train to the dentist's waiting room. The board and cards pack flat and, for older children, all you need is a pencil and paper.

Weaving box

Three to five years

At three, your child probably won't be dextrous enough to use a sewing needle, but weaving does not demand such accuracy and is a fun craft to start him off with, while developing better hand-eye co-ordination.

By having six separate pieces of different coloured wool, knotted at both ends of the box, as the warp, and changing the colour of the weft every ten rows or so, he can make a piece of really attractive multi-coloured woven material. When he has finished, you could make it into a small bag or purse.

Right craft, right child
Some children can make origami creatures by the time they are four and sew passably by five. Others are still all fingers and thumbs. Practice plays a big part, but so does seeing other members of the family enjoying craftwork. It is no coincidence that such skills were passed down from parent to child. If you are not 'setting a good example' the trick is to choose the right craft and the right time.

Not just fun but

★ Teaches the child to work towards an end.
★ Teaches the child to work by himself.
★ Teaches the child to sit still and concentrate.
★ Good for hand-eye co-ordination.
★ Sense of achievement boosts confidence.

To make this simple weaving box, punch six holes at each end of a shoe box, and thread a long piece of wool through all the holes, tying one knot before you start and one after the last hole. The wool should form six taut lines (the warp). Wind another long piece of wool – the end result will look particularly attractive if this is a different colour – around a piece of cardboard.

Tie the end of this piece of wool around the first line of wool in the box and then show him how to weave across the warp, over one line and under the next, to produce the weft. If he finishes the piece of wool he's using as the weft before the end, knot another piece on to the original.

Tip tap shapes

Four years on

This game is perfect for children who enjoy doing things with their hands. You will need a square or rectangular cork tile mounted on a stiff piece of backing board. Or use any material, such as chipboard or fibreboard, soft enough to take pins.

Cut out various shapes from different coloured card – triangles, circles, semi-circles, trapeziums, rectangles, squares and long and short stick shapes. You'll also need a small hammer and a box of pinboard pins.

Not just fun but

★ Teaches the child to work towards an end.
★ Teaches the child to work by herself.
★ Good for hand-eye co-ordination.
★ Good for spatial skills.

As the shapes are only attached to the board by a central pin, they can be moved. She can experiment by arranging a series of shapes into a pattern and then seeing which ones she can move. Sometimes there will be a knock-on effect, so that the whole pattern will move when she touches one shape.

To fix a shape to the board, she must tap a pin through the centre of the card with the little hammer. You should supervise this game to ensure that she doesn't prick herself with the pins or hit her thumb with the hammer. Show her how to arrange the shapes to make a picture.

Two triangles could be the roof of a house, the outside, made with long stick shapes, the windows, squares, and the door, short stick shapes with a semi-circular fanlight. A circle could be the head of a bird, its beak, two short stick shapes, its body, a trapezium, two more short stick shapes for its legs, and its tail, a long triangle. Cars, trucks, buses and trains are also easy to make from the shapes.

Cork people
Collect corks, from wine bottles, cut them in half and let the child fix these to the board. They can be put together to make animals and people. If you have enough corks you can make an attractive notice board by sticking them to the board in lines.

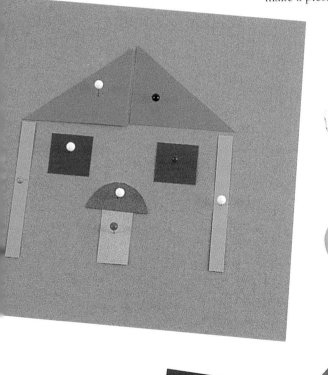

Shoe box theatre

Four to five years

This is an elaborate 'little world' game for a child who likes to entertain and who has the hand skills to manage one or two puppets. Use finger puppets or hand puppets for the younger children and glove puppets when they are more skilled (page 34).

Decorate finger puppets with faces and hair and add little caps of paper or felt. Alternatively you could draw faces on wooden spoons, glue on some wool for hair and make a material cape to cover the handle.

Not just fun but

★ Putting on a show makes children feel important.
★ Playing different roles helps the child understand about self and other and challenges memory.
★ Good for fine finger movements.

Make the theatre from a fairly large shoe box or, if she's doing it with a friend, an even larger cardboard box. Discard the lid and cut out one of the long sides, leaving a frame of a few centimetres all the way round.

From the spare cardboard, make a decoration to stick above the open side to form a proscenium arch. Be sure to have the open top of the shoe box as the bottom of your theatre. Help her to paint the box with poster paints and make a backdrop by painting a picture on a piece of paper and glueing it inside. Use small pieces of fabric taped in place as curtains.

When she stages her show, cover a table with a cloth and place the theatre at the edge, taped firmly on to the cloth with masking tape, so that the back of the box over-hangs the table and gives her room for her puppets. Tell her to crouch down below the top of the table, and shine a light on to the stage.

As well as a theatre, a box can be a variety of other things, such as a garage, a dollshouse or an aquarium. To make an aquarium, cut the side out of a shoe box just as you did for the theatre, but keep the lid on. Paint the outside and then decorate the inside with an underwater scene – a sandy seabed for the bottom and some seaweed creeping up the sides. Cut out card fish and the odd octopus, attach a short piece of cotton thread to each one and tape it to the inside of the lid, so they dangle down.

Musical statues

Four to five years

Children can feel rhythm and enjoy music long before they can produce it. Encourage your child to dance along to CDs or music on the radio – whatever is playing, pop, jazz, classical music, nursery rhymes or dance music. Give her some ideas. If it's a march, suggest that she is a soldier; if it's gentle, a fairy or snowflake; if it's a slow piece, a sleepy dormouse; if it's fast and furious, a flickering flame. To give structure to these sessions, especially if there is a group of children, play 'Musical statues'.

Another musical game you could play is that old favourite 'musical chairs'. Set up a row of chairs, (or cushions) with one less chair than the number of children. Play the music as in 'Musical statues', stopping it from time to time. The children dance around the chairs and when the music stops, they all make a dash to sit down. The one child who is left without a chair goes out. For the next round, you remove one more chair. The game continues until there is one chair and two children to fight over it. Musical chairs is noisier and requires more space than 'Musical statues'.

You take charge of the music for the game, and explain to the children how you will keep stopping it, at which point you want them to freeze. Any child who carries on moving has to go out. The only child who remains in at the end is the winner. Choose the music carefully so that you can suggest themes around which the children might base their dancing.

Musical statues is a great game for parties. It will quieten a rowdy gang of children very effectively. It doesn't have to be reserved for parties though. The game is excellent for sharpening the children's reactions and improving muscle control. Freezing and remaining frozen has to be controlled and is much more difficult than moving or dancing.

Not just fun but

★ Encourages listening and musical skills.

★ Starting and stopping provides excellent exercise.

★ Rushing about improves spatial skills.

★ Helps muscle control.

Chinese whispers

Four to five years

To play 'Chinese whispers' successfully, you need at least three children, preferably more. It comes into its own when children get over-excited at parties: drop it in between boisterous games.

Seat them in a circle on the floor. Think up a sentence, which is simple but contains a variety of sounds, like 'The fox is playing his xylophone today', or 'The teacher scrapes her chalk on the blackboard', or 'Sally Smith wants to eat peanuts on the picnic'. If they are younger than four, you could make the sentences even simpler: 'The black cat ran away', 'The dog's gnawing on a bone', 'The circus is coming to town'. Whisper the sentence to one of the children (so quietly that the others can't hear), who then whispers it to the next child and so on, until the last child has to speak aloud the sentence that he has just heard. Afterwards you can tell the children what your original sentence was, and compare the two. The greater the difference between them, the more amusing it will be.

Once they've played a few rounds of the game, or if the children are older, they can invent their own sentences.

Making pom poms

Four years on

Your child might not be quite dextrous enough to start sewing with a needle, but by the age of four, she should be capable of tackling a pom pom. It might not be quite so common to have a pom pom on a hat as it was once, but she will enjoy creating something round, fluffy and colourful from objects as unpromising as circles of card and pieces of wool.

To give your pom pom an even more colourful appearance, use wool with a twist of different colours, or change colours several times as you make it, knotting the end of one piece of wool to the beginning of the new piece.

Not just fun but

★ Sense of achievement. Pom poms look so much better than you think they will.

★ Fine finger skills.

★ Working towards an end.

★ Encourages the child to sit still.

It's simple

Draw two large identical circles on a piece of card and cut them both out. Mark a smaller circle inside each of the card circles and cut these out too. Place the two card circles together. Take a ball of wool – it mustn't be too large, or it won't go through the inner circle – and start working your way around the circles by threading the wool through the hole in the centre. Continue to do this until there is no hole left to push the wool through. Tie off the end of the wool, and carefully cut around the edge of the woollen circle. Pull the card templates away and fluff up your new pom pom.

The weather man

Four to five years

Children of this age are usually disinterested in the weather unless it's raining so heavily that they are prevented from going out to play. Inventing an activity centred around the weather might spark your child's interest, and although he will still be too young to understand what causes meterological changes, he will soon recognize that the weather doesn't just happen. Watch the weather forecast with him on television, point out the various symbols, and then keep an eye on the weather itself to see if the forecast was right.

	Morning	Noon	Evening
Monday			
Tuesday			
Wednesday			
Thursday			
Friday			
Saturday			
Sunday			

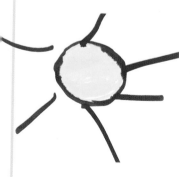

Weather chart

Make a wall chart for the week, with three columns for each day. He can draw simple illustrations in the boxes, or you can cut out a number of squares of card or paper and ask him to draw symbols on each one: sun, clouds, rain, snowflakes, and perhaps a fluttering flag to symbolize wind. You could write the words, 'sun', 'cloud', 'rain', 'snow' and 'wind' underneath the drawings. Record the weather every day with him when he gets up in the morning, at noon and in the early evening before it gets dark. Stick the appropriate card on the chart with some Blu-Tack.

He will probably be fascinated by the changes and start taking notice of the weather independently. Encourage him to stick the cards on the chart by himself.

Rain gauge

If he enjoys this activity, you could make a simple rain gauge together and add coloured stickers to represent the rain readings to your chart. All you need to make the gauge is a tall, thin collecting jar and a wide funnel, which will guarantee that even small quantities of rain will be collected. At this stage, don't mark the jar with centimetres, but paint different coloured lines up the side of it, and don't forget to have a colour for zero rainfall. It is best to record rainfall during a time of the year when the weather is changeable as the variations will interest him. Take your readings from the jar at the same time every day and add a coloured sticker to your wall chart. The sticker should be the same colour as the line on the jar nearest the rain level.

Not just fun but

★ Simple science.
★ Generates plenty of questions.
★ Something to show his friends.
★ A quiet activity for a rainy day.
★ Chart making helps the child to work towards an end.
★ Chart making is a quiet activity.
★ Doing things together encourages conversation.
★ Teaches the child to follow instructions.

Making masks

Four to five years

Faces hold a deep fascination for children almost from the moment they are born, and masks combine this fascination with an element of make-believe. You can buy masks, but it is much more fun for children to make their own. Younger children can make simple masks from a large paper bag – you put the bag over the head, mark where the eye holes are to be, and decorate it as you like with a felt-tipped pen. (Bear in mind that some children do not like things put over their heads, and of course plastic bags must NEVER be used.)

Not just fun but

★ Can help the child confront his fears.
★ Helps the child to work towards an end.
★ Requires the child to pay attention and watch carefully.
★ Helps the child to understand that things must be done in the right order.
★ A quiet activity.
★ Doing things together encourages conversation.
★ Teaches the child to follow instructions.
★ Sustained activity.

Older children can make more elaborate masks from card, rolled into a tube and joined with tape or elastic at the back. You can make eye holes in the mouth and draw in fake eyes higher up, which makes the mask much bigger and more impressive. Make masks for yourself and the rest of the family as well, so that it becomes a shared game (see 'Paper plate faces', page 132).

Suggest themes for the masks: a happy face, sad face, angry face, funny face, prince, princess, clown, monster, any favourite animal.

A few ideas for middle and later childhood games and activities are suggested in this short section. They range from craft activities, magic tricks and simple scientific experiments to word and board games.

Five Years On

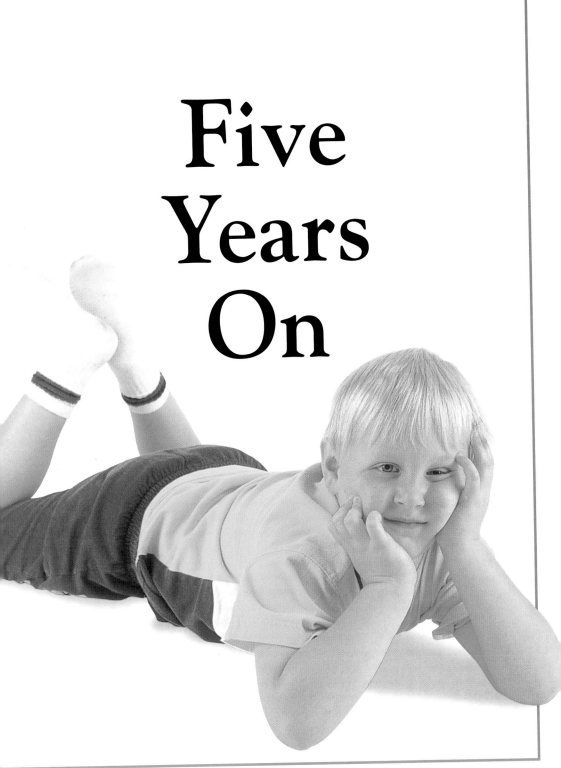

Magic tricks

Five years on

Most five-year-olds are intrigued by magic tricks and love to put on shows for their friends and relations in which they are the principal performers. The problem is that most tricks are too difficult for them to attempt at this age. Here, however, are a few ideas for very simple tricks, which can be almost guaranteed to work every time.

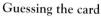

Levitating wand

For the first trick, your child will need a magic wand. If he doesn't have one, you could make one from a piece of dowel, covered in black sticky paper with white painted tips. He can tell his audience that this trick proves that the wand is magic. He holds the wand in the palm of his right hand with his fingers curled over it and the back of this hand to the audience. He grips his right wrist with his left hand, the back of his left hand facing him. He opens the fingers of his right hand. As if by magic, the wand does not fall to the floor because – and the others won't realize this – he has used his left forefinger to support it.

Guessing the card

The second trick is a standard card trick, but easy enough for a five-year-old to master. He takes a pack of cards, asks a member of the audience to pick one. While he examines this card, the little magician can surreptitiously look at the card that was above it in the pack. He then puts the picked card back in its place, and starts turning over the pack, card by card, until he comes to the card he has seen. He knows the picked card follows it, and can display it.

★ Encourages the child
to look for another
explanation.
★ Social game.
★ Encourages the child
to organize an activity.

★ Learning
that magic is
sometimes not
magic.

Disappearing coin
For the final trick, he needs
a plastic glass, a coin and a
thick paper cone, all placed
on a large piece of white
paper covering a low table.
He tells his audience that
he is going to make
the coin disappear. He
places the cone over the
glass and then both
over the coin. Then,
'Abracadabra', he lifts
the cone off, leaving
the glass but no coin
visible underneath it.
The secret is that earlier
he will have stuck a circle
of white paper, exactly
the same size as the glass,
to its rim. To make the
coin reappear, he simply
puts the cone back over the
glass and lifts both off.
'Abracadabra', the coin is
revealed.

*Help him to dress
the part, with a
cape and a black
conical hat made from
thick paper or thin
card and decorated
with silver stars.*

Candle making

Five years on

As a treat children love to have the occasional meal, bath or story by candlelight. Rather than using manufactured candles, your child will be even more delighted if she has made them herself, although you will need to heat the wax and generally oversee the activity.

Before you start candle making, look out a metal jam-jar lid and put it in the freezer. Next you need a tube of thin cardboard (the inside of a toilet roll is perfect, unless you want a particularly long thin or short fat candle, in which case you'll have to make the tube yourself). Make four holes in the tube, two opposite each other one centimetre from the top, and two opposite each other one centimetre from the bottom. Insert one cocktail stick through the holes at the top and one through the holes at the bottom, so they form bars across the inside of the tube. Tie a piece of wick around the top stick, leaving a few centimetres dangling over the edge of the tube. Pull the wick tight and knot it around the bottom stick before cutting it.

While she grates a wax crayon in any colour she chooses, you melt 120 grams of paraffin wax or used candle ends in a saucepan over a low heat until it is liquid. Retrieve the lid from the freezer and stand the cardboard tube on it. Then pour the hot wax from the pan into the tube, a little at a time. As it touches the cold lid, it will start to set and be prevented from running out of the bottom of the tube. Leave the wax to cool for a couple of hours before cutting off the tube and trimming the wick.

Not just fun but

★ Helps the child to work towards an end.

★ Requires the child to pay attention and watch carefully.

★ Teaches the child not to rush at things.

★ Doing things together encourages conversation.

★ Teaches the child to follow instructions.

With stripes

When you and she have made several candles, you could experiment with making striped ones. The instructions are exactly the same, except that you must heat up as many pans of wax as you want different coloured stripes in your candle. Before you start pouring, mark the tube at the points where you want the stripes to finish so that you get them the right depth. Pour the first colour in to the tube and let it set for a few minutes, then pour in the second colour, and so on. A sequence of colours repeated looks particularly stunning, and these candles make terrific presents.

Make a pinwheel

Five years on

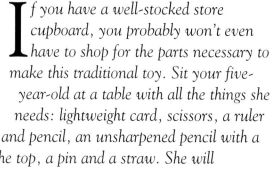

*I*f you have a well-stocked store cupboard, you probably won't even have to shop for the parts necessary to make this traditional toy. Sit your five-year-old at a table with all the things she needs: lightweight card, scissors, a ruler and pencil, an unsharpened pencil with a rubber at the top, a pin and a straw. She will undoubtedly want to make the pinwheel by herself, but you will need to be on hand to help from time to time.

Encourage her to decorate her pinwheel with stickers or her own pictures on the four remaining points.

Not just fun but

★ Introduces trial and error.
★ Making something that works is always special.

Cut the paper to form a ten centimetre square, then draw two diagonal lines from the bottom corners to the top corners. The point where the lines bisect is the centre. Measure two centimetres from the centre along the diagonal lines in all four directions, and mark with a pencil. Then cut along the diagonal lines towards the centre from each corner, stopping at the pencil mark.

You now have eight pointed edges. Lift one up just past the centre and push the pin through the point (not the centre). Miss out the next point, but bring up the one after and follow with the two other alternate points, tucking them all under the first one and fixing them with the pin. Press the pin through the centre of the card to complete the wheel.

Cut one centimetre off the end of the straw and thread the pin through it, so that it acts as a separator. Push the pin into the rubber at the end of the pencil and then bend the pin over so that the straw separator is at right angles to the pencil and your pinwheel can spin freely.

Tie dyeing

Five years on

Other ways to decorate clothes
are with special fabric pens or
paints. Your child can either
paint free-hand pictures or
make patterned
impressions with
printing
blocks (see
page 102).

This idea
was born
in the 1960s
at the height of 'flower
power', but tie-dyed T-shirts
have recently re-emerged as fashion items, and you
and your child will be fascinated by the dyeing process.
You will need to buy a cold-water dye or, if you want
a blend of colours, buy two. Set up a 'messy' corner,
cover the surface on which you will be working with a
plastic sheet or newspapers, and dress yourselves in
aprons or overalls. The process works best on cotton,
so if you just want to experiment, use a piece of old
sheet, but if you want to cheer up some clothes, a
plain white cotton T-shirt is ideal.

Not just fun but

★ Helps the child to work
towards an end.
★ Requires the child to pay
attention and watch
carefully.
★ Helps the child to
understand that things must
be done in the right order.
★ A quiet activity.
★ Doing things together
encourages conversation.
★ Teaches the child to
follow instructions.
★ Sustained activity.

The technique
Every 15 or 20 centimetres,
bunch up the cloth all over
the garment and tie string
tightly around the bunched-
up part. The string will
prevent the dye from
penetrating the material that
it covers. To create an
interesting 'starburst' effect,
tie stones into the cloth.

Using the manufacturer's
instructions, mix up one
colour – ideally in a large
preserving pan or enamel
bowl – and dye the garment.
Then rinse it very
thoroughly. For an even more
colourful effect, repeat the
tie-dyeing with a different
colour dye.

Sewing

Five years on

B y five, your child should have the finger control to start some simple sewing, and be old enough to use a needle, albeit a large blunt one and under adult supervision. Start her off with sewing cards. You can make these easily by drawing a simple, stylized picture on a piece of card and punching holes along the outline. Keep the outline near the edge of the card because she'll find it hard to sew near the middle. Alternatively cut out your picture.

Thread a darning or tapestry needle for her with a piece of coloured wool. If the wool slips easily through the needle, double it. Knot the wool and demonstrate how to stitch in and out of the punched holes. Then try punching holes without drawing a picture, so that she won't know what it is until she has finished sewing. She can progress from cards on to fabric: Binca at first, then tapestry canvas and then felt.

Not just fun but

★ Fine finger skills.
★ Working towards an end.
★ Encourages the child to sit still.
★ Useful life skill.

★ Sense of achievement.
★ Good activity for a confined space such as a aeroplane.

Salt and pepper

Six years on

At six your child's appetite for information will be voracious, and conducting simple scientific experiments such as this one, which also has an appealing element of 'magic', will fascinate him. Mix a couple of teaspoonfuls of salt and pepper together. Then give him a spoon and ask him to separate them. This is an impossible task unless you know the secret.

Not just fun but

★ Simple science.
★ Generates lots of questions.

★ Something to show his friends.
★ A quiet activity for a rainy day.

Although not so magical as the salt and pepper experiment, a simple game which will entrance a younger child is to fill a glass with warm water and add a spoonful of sugar. Let her stir it with a teaspoon and watch the sugar dissolve in the water.

The secret is to rub the spoon vigorously against a jumper or other article of clothing made of man-made fabric or silk and place it above the salt and pepper mixture. The lightness of the pepper means that the static electricity will lift it up from the mixture, leaving the salt behind. He could incorporate this 'trick' into his magic show (see page 164).

This demonstration of the power of static electricity will seem like pure magic to young children, while older ones will begin to understand an essential scientific principle.

Invisible ink

Seven to nine years

This is a game for those secret years when children traditionally played outdoors and thought their parents did not know where they were or what they were doing. Sadly many children no longer have the opportunity to roam the streets, woods and fields. They can have some secrets none the less. Along with dens and passwords comes writing in invisible ink.

By the age of seven, a child will probably be intrigued by the idea of communicating secretly. He might invent a password to be given before entering his room, and he and a friend could spend many happy hours playing secret games together.

Invisible ink for recording the password can be made simply from potato juice, with the potato as inkwell. Take a large potato and cut off the top and bottom. Stand it upright and scoop out a hole in the top. With a knife, scrape off the excess liquid from the cut pieces of potato into the hole.

Dip a used matchstick into the potato juice in the hole and use it to write on a piece of plain white paper. When it dries, the ink will be totally invisible, and will only reappear if he heats the paper for a few minutes in a low oven, set at 125 degrees centigrade. He could also use lemon juice, onion juice or Coca-Cola for invisible ink, and should treat them and heat them in exactly the same way as potato juice.

With wax

Another way of writing secret messages is with wax. He should rub a sheet of paper with a wax candle, then place the paper wax-side down on top of another sheet. If he writes firmly on the paper, his words will be pressed in wax on to the sheet beneath. To read the message, he should sprinkle coloured powder, fine-grain instant coffee for example, on to the paper.

Not just fun but

★ Secret societies encourage children to see themselves as part of a group outside the family.

★ Simple science.

★ Generates plenty of questions.

★ Something to show his friends.

★ A quiet activity for a rainy day.

Scissors, paper, stone

Seven years on

This old Japanese game called Jan-Ken-Pon, known in the West as 'Scissors, paper, stone', is a brilliant way for a couple of children to while away ten or 15 minutes, particularly if they're waiting, in a confined space, or on a journey. There are several different versions of the game. The best known, shown here, is for the two children to hold one hand behind their backs. Together they say, 'One, two, three', then they have to bring their hands in front of them, formed into one of three shapes: scissors, where the forefinger and middle finger are extended sideways into a scissor-shape; paper, where the hand is held out flat; and stone, where the child makes a fist. The children compare shapes. Scissors beat paper because they cut it. Paper beats stone because it wraps it. Stone beats scissors because it blunts them.

As the children get into the rhythm of the game, they can increase the speed. It should be played fast, and there's no need to keep the score.

Not just fun but

★ A good way of settling disputes or deciding who goes first.
★ Improves co-ordination.
★ Makes a child think fast.
★ Anticipation.

Tic tac toe

Seven years on

L ike 'Scissors, paper, stone' (see page 173), this is a game with an ancient heritage which is easy to learn and will occupy two children for hours on a wet afternoon. It is played on a board, which you can draw yourself on paper or, better still, card. The board consists of three boxes. Draw the first box two or three centimetres square. The second box should be twice the size of the first and contain it. The third box should be one and a half times the size of the second and contain both. Add four straight lines from the middle of each side of the smallest box to the middle of each side of the largest box, which will bisect the sides of the middle box. Give both players three counters each.

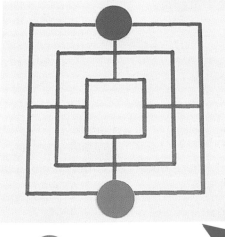

Not just fun but

★ Teaches the children to be good winners and losers.
★ Introduces the concept of strategy.

To play, the children must take it in turns to put a counter on the board at an intersection until they both have their three counters in play, at which point they can move one counter to an adjacent intersection on their turn. Their aim is to achieve a straight line of three counters, while preventing their opponent from gaining one.

Unlike other board games, this one can be played almost anywhere.

Categories

Five to ten years

The idea that things belong to families – or categories – is something with which six-year-olds are normally just coming to terms. This game, like 'Odd man out' (see page 50), is designed to help your child become familiar with some of these categories as well as categories within categories.

(see page 50)

Not just fun but

★ Grouping things together is another pre-maths skill.
★ Encourages simple logic.
★ Prepares child for simple scientific principles.

When she begins to find this game too easy, try her on categories within categories – marsupials, deciduous trees, wild flowers, and an African country.

	A	B	C
Item of clothing			
Type of food			

To start with, think of a category, like birds or insects, trees or flowers, colours or shapes, to get the ball rolling. She must then come up with something in that category. If she finds it hard, you could start or give her a few clues to help her. When she has thought of something that belongs to your category, switch roles and ask her to choose a category for you.

For a younger child, make the categories extremely basic: an animal, a drink, something to eat, an article of clothing. To make it really difficult for an older child, give her the category and then say whatever it is has to start with a specific letter of the alphabet.

More challenging...
By the time she can write, you can expand the game. She can play alone or with friends. They must all have a pencil and paper with approximately ten or 12 categories written on it, then choose a letter of the alphabet and see how many of the categories they can cover in a timed period.

Acknowledgements

Models

Harry Armstrong
Jess Armstrong
Megan Armstrong
Dyandria Baugh
Tia Eno
Franny Glass
Georgia Graham
Alex Hughes
Nia Hughes
Turab Iqbal
Alex Keene
Lorraine Keene
Ella Kendal-Peel
Harry Sprunt
Oliver Sprunt
Jordan Stewart

Photography Dave Armstrong
Editorial director Andrew Duncan
Assistant editors Leo Glass, Nicola Davies
Proof reader Sharon van der Merwe
Art director Mel Petersen
Designer Beverley Stewart